2ND EDITION

One Pot Meals

for People with Diabetes

RUTH GLICK and NANCY BAGGETT

American Diabetes Association.

Cure • Care • Commitment®

Managing Editor, Book Publishing, Abe Ogden; *Acquisitions Editor, Consumer Books,* Robert Anthony; *Production Manager,* Melissa Sprott; *Composition,* American Diabetes Association; *Cover Design,* VC Graphics; *Printer,* Transcontinental Printing.

Printed in Canada
1 3 5 7 9 10 8 6 4 2

The suggestions and information contained in this publication are generally consistent with the *Clinical Practice Recommendations* and other policies of the American Diabetes Association, but they do not represent the policy or position of the Association or any of its boards or committees. Reasonable steps have been taken to ensure the accuracy of the information presented. However, the American Diabetes Association cannot ensure the safety or efficacy of any product or service described in this publication. Individuals are advised to consult a physician or other appropriate health care professional before undertaking any diet or exercise program or taking any medication referred to in this publication. Professionals must use and apply their own professional judgment, experience, and training and should not rely solely on the information contained in this publication before prescribing any diet, exercise, or medication. The American Diabetes Association—its officers, directors, employees, volunteers, and members—assumes no responsibility or liability for personal or other injury, loss, or damage that may result from the suggestions or information in this publication.

∞ The paper in this publication meets the requirements of the ANSI Standard Z39.48-1992 (permanence of paper).

ADA titles may be purchased for business or promotional use or for special sales. To purchase more than 50 copies of this book at a discount, or for custom editions of this book with your logo, contact Lee Romano Sequeira, Special Sales & Promotions, at the address below, or at LRomano@diabetes.org or 703-299-2046.

For all other inquiries, please call 1-800-DIABETES.

American Diabetes Association
1701 North Beauregard Street
Alexandria, Virginia 22311

Library of Congress Cataloging-in-Publication Data

Glick, Ruth, 1942-
  One pot meals for people with diabetes / Ruth Glick and Nancy Baggett. — 2nd ed.
    p. cm.
  Includes bibliographical references and index.
  ISBN 978-1-58040-263-7 (alk. paper)
  1. Diabetes—Diet therapy—Recipes. 2. Quick and easy cookery. 3. One-dish meals. I. Baggett, Nancy, 1943- II. Title.

  RC662.G59 2007
  641.5'6314—dc22

            2007007953

CONTENTS

INTRODUCTION

At the end of a long day, nothing beats a good, home-cooked meal for taste appeal and nutritional value. Yet in today's busy world, it's harder and harder to find the time to cook dinner from scratch.

That's why we love one-dish meals. They're a wonderful way to get a whole dinner on the table without a lot of fuss. They offer interesting and varied combinations of flavors and textures. They lend themselves to quick cleanup and, sometimes, yummy leftovers, too!

In *One Pot Meals* we feature 150 well-tested, one-dish meals, in chapters including skillet dinners, stews and hot pots, pasta-and-sauce combos, oven dinners, microwave specials, slow-cooker meals, hearty sandwiches and wraps, and even savory meal-in-a-bowl salads. Some of our recipes, such as Turkey and Dumplings, Chicken Cacciatore, and Manhattan-Style Clam Chowder, are old favorites presented here in healthier form. Others, such as Sesame-Noodle Stir-Fry with Chicken, Tilapia with Olives and Artichokes, and Basil-Chive Pesto and Pasta, are completely new options that aim to expand your range and repertoire. All make tasty eating, so give them a try!

Realizing that most cooks today are time-pressed, we've included chapters on "super-quick" dinners and hurry-up microwave dishes in the book. Even more important, we've streamlined *all* our recipes as much as possible. Ingredients and preparation time are kept to a minimum, and most dishes are ready in 30 minutes or less, though the slow-cooker meals and some oven meals take longer. However, they're designed so you can put them together quickly, then leave them to finish cooking on their own.

But there's another appealing and even more important feature of this book; it makes it easy to serve both truly tempting *and* healthful fare. Drawing on our years of experience developing good and good-for-you recipes, we've incorporated taste-pleasing herbs, spices, and other seasonings with a wealth of vegetables, whole grains, and legumes, and with meat in the right proportion to fit with the current American Diabetes Association recommendations. (In fact, providing easy, tasty ways to increase consumption of good-for-you vegetables was one of our key goals in the book.) Plus, we've been mindful of the guidelines on dietary fat, cholesterol, and sodium. (All the hard numbers are provided in the nutritional analysis accompanying each dish.)

Fat intake is always an important dietary issue, but because diabetes is a risk factor for heart disease, it's especially important to your health to be careful about fat consumption. You may have noticed that there's been a shift over the past few years in dietary thinking about fats. Previously, many nutrition experts urged that recipes should contain as little fat as possible. Now there's a growing recognition that some fats are healthier than others, and that it's more important to limit fat from certain meat and dairy products than from olive and canola oils, fish, nuts, and seeds. Some consumption of fat from these latter sources is even encouraged.

So, throughout this book, we've limited animal fat both by controlling the amount of meat in recipes and by using lean cuts such as skinless chicken breasts and extra-lean ground beef. We also specifically call for reduced-fat milk and cheese products or cheeses, such as feta, that are naturally lower in fat than other varieties. Where fats are needed for flavor and to facilitate cooking, we rely heavily on olive oil, a monounsaturated fat that may help lower cholesterol. Nuts are also rich in unsaturated fats that help lower cholesterol (and are a major source of certain vitamins and minerals), so we call for these in some dishes, too. And we've included many recipes that feature salmon and other fish high in omega three fatty acids, which also have been shown to lower cholesterol in many individuals.

We didn't try to make our recipes fat-free for still another reason—removing all the fat often removes all the taste! And fine flavor is always our bottom line. No matter how healthful it is, if food doesn't taste good, nobody will eat it—which, of course, defeats the purpose of cooking at all. We've kept this fact in focus while creating all our recipes.

Carbohydrates are another component of the diet we've kept in mind. As you probably know, whole grains are better for you than highly refined grains. That's why we call for whole-wheat bread in recipes that use bread and why we suggest using brown rice instead of white. (Since brown rice requires an extended cooking time, we recommend preparing it ahead and keeping it in the freezer until needed. You can also purchase quick-cooking brown rice or packages of ready-to-serve brown rice.)

The recipes in *One Pot Meals* also take into account the need to moderate sodium intake. Throughout the book, we've built in salt-saving steps, such as always rinsing canned beans before using them (which removes a significant amount of excess salt), and stretching small quantities of salty ingredients such as olives and pickles by chopping them. In a number of recipes, we also direct you to taste the finished dish before adding any salt, which helps avoid inadvertent overuse. Additionally, we always call for lower-sodium "lite" soy sauce and reduced-sodium chicken broth, and in many recipes we also recommend using less-salty versions of ingredients such as canned tomatoes and tomato sauce. Note that wherever recipes do include a choice of ingredients, *their nutritional analysis is always based on the first choice mentioned.*

To help you stay within your diet plan, we clearly indicate portion sizes in *One Pot Meals.* If your meal plan allows you to eat more, you can always take a bigger portion. Just remember to count the extra amount in your total food intake. And check the nutritional analysis provided with each recipe, so you'll know the exchanges along with the calories, cholesterol, fat, and other important information.

We're proud of this collection of one-dish meals. We've taste-tested them all on family, friends, and colleagues and refined recipes in response to their feedback. Everything here has earned an enthusiastic reception.

So the next time you're wondering what to fix for dinner, thumb through the pages of this book, and pick something new to try. There are recipes to satisfy a variety of tastes, fit a variety of schedules, and, best of all, enable you to turn out a spectacular assortment of healthful and mouth-watering one-pot meals.

SLOW-COOKER PRIMER

We've discovered that, while slow-cooker cooking is easy and convenient, in some ways it's quite different from most other familiar methods. Here are some basic principles to keep in mind:

- All slow-cooker recipes are designed to be cooked with the lid in place. Moreover, these meals can be left unattended for long periods; frequent lifting of the lid usually causes significant heat loss and may lengthen cooking time.

- Due to the fitted lid and low cooking temperatures (even with the "high" setting), less water than normal evaporates from slow-cooker recipes. In some cases, this means that recipes call for bouillon cubes or granules with a disproportionately small amount of water. This boosts flavor and keeps the broth from becoming too diluted as the meat and vegetables exude their juices. In other instances, recipes simply call for less liquid than the dish appears to need at the start because we know from experience it will have plenty by the end of cooking.

■ Slow-cooker cooking changes the taste of food in unpredictable ways. Bay leaves, for example, often tend to taste stronger at the end of the cooking period, while the flavor of chili powder sometimes becomes less pronounced. As a result, don't go by the amounts of seasonings you're used to adding in a conventional recipe, and don't make seasoning adjustments until a dish is done.

■ Slow cookers come in a variety of sizes and with varied features. Since the large majority of models contain only low and high settings and have a 2 1/2- to 3-quart capacity, most of our recipes are designed to accommodate these. If you have a super-size pot or one with multiple heat settings, the recipes will still work fine, though of course they won't take full advantage of your appliance.

■ Slow cookers vary considerably in individual cooking temperatures and efficiency. While we have timed the cooking periods for all our recipes, they may cook faster or slower in your model. When cooking raw meat, it's important to start off on the high setting for an hour. After that, it's perfectly all right to stretch out or cut down cooking time to fit your own schedule by choosing a setting yourself. As a rough guideline, the high setting gets things done in half the time of the low setting.

Super-Quick Dinners

ITALIAN CHICKEN WITH PEPPERS AND ONIONS

Here's an easy but delicious Italian chicken dinner featuring several convenience items: frozen pepper and onion stir-fry, seasoned tomato sauce, and minced garlic.

> 1 Tbsp olive oil
>
> 1 tsp minced garlic
>
> 3/4 lb boneless, skinless chicken breast, cut into bite-sized pieces
>
> 2 cups Italian-seasoned tomato sauce
>
> 3 cups frozen mixed pepper and onion stir-fry (thawed)
>
> Salt and pepper to taste (optional)
>
> 1 1/2 cups penne or similar pasta, cooked according to package directions without added salt or fat
>
> 2 Tbsp grated Parmesan cheese

1 In a large, nonstick skillet, combine the oil and garlic. Add the chicken, and cook over medium heat, stirring frequently, until the chicken begins to brown, about 4 to 5 minutes.

2 Add the tomato sauce. Stir in the pepper and onions. Bring to a boil. Reduce heat, cover, and simmer, stirring occasionally, about 12 to 15 minutes, until the chicken is cooked through. Stir in the pasta. Sprinkle with Parmesan cheese. Serve from skillet.

PREP TIME: **10** MINUTES

SERVINGS: **4**

SERVING SIZE: **1 1/2** CUPS

Exchanges
2 1/2 Starch
2 Vegetable
2 Lean Meat

Calories 372
   Calories from Fat 72
Total Fat . . . . .8 g
   Saturated Fat . . . . .1 g
Cholesterol . . . . .52 mg
Sodium . . . . .597 mg
Total Carbohydrate . . . .46 g
   Dietary Fiber . . . . .2 g
   Sugars . . . . .11 g
Protein . . . . .29 g

SOUTH-OF-THE-BORDER CHICKEN SKILLET

"Chicken takes on spicy flavor in this super-quick skillet dinner."

1 lb boneless, skinless chicken breast, cut into bite-sized pieces
1 medium green bell pepper, seeded and diced
1 tsp minced garlic
1 Tbsp olive oil
3/4 cup mild salsa
3/4 cup water
1 15-oz can kidney beans, rinsed and drained
1 tsp chili powder, or to taste
1/4 tsp salt
1/2 cup quick-cooking rice

PREP TIME: 10 MINUTES

SERVINGS: 4

SERVING SIZE: 1 CUP

Exchanges
1 1/2 Starch
1 Vegetable
4 Very Lean Meat
1/2 Fat

Calories 323
  Calories from Fat 59
Total Fat . . . . .7 g
  Saturated Fat . . . . . . .2 g
Cholesterol . . . . .68 mg
Sodium . . . . .461 mg
Total Carbohydrate . . . .32 g
  Dietary Fiber . . . . . . .6 g
  Sugars . . . . .4 g
Protein . . . . .33 g

1 In a large nonstick skillet, cook the chicken, pepper, and garlic in oil over medium heat, stirring frequently, until the chicken turns white, about 6 to 8 minutes.

2 Add the salsa, water, kidney beans, chili powder, and salt. Cover and bring to a boil. Reduce the heat, and simmer 10 to 12 minutes.

3 Bring to a boil. Add the rice, and stir into sauce. Cover, remove pan from heat, and allow to sit until rice is tender, about 5 minutes.

HOT-CHA-CHA TURKEY SKILLET PRONTO

This is a slightly spicy dinner, but it can be tailored to your taste. For just a little heat, use a mild salsa or picante sauce; for more fire, use a medium-hot version. Also, to keep the dish relatively tame, be sure to use mild green chiles.

4 4-oz turkey breast cutlets

1/2 cup mild or medium-hot salsa or picante sauce, divided

3/4 tsp mild or medium chili powder

1/2 tsp ground allspice

1 Tbsp olive oil

1 medium onion, coarsely chopped

1 4-oz can chopped mild green chiles, well drained

1 14-oz package frozen (thawed) corn, black bean, and sweet pepper medley

1/4 cup chopped cilantro or parsley leaves, plus extra for garnish (optional)

Salt and black pepper to taste (optional)

PREP TIME: 15 MINUTES

SERVINGS: 4

SERVING SIZE: 4-OZ CUTLET, PLUS 3/4 CUP CORN-BEAN MIXTURE

Exchanges
1 Starch
1 Vegetable
4 Very Lean Meat
1/2 Fat

Calories	270
Calories from Fat	35
Total Fat	4 g
Saturated Fat	1 g
Cholesterol	73 mg
Sodium	338 mg
Total Carbohydrate	18 g
Dietary Fiber	8 g
Sugars	6 g
Protein	32 g

1 In a medium non-reactive bowl, stir together the turkey cutlets, 1/4 cup salsa, chili powder, and allspice. Let stand for 5 minutes.

2 In a 12-inch nonstick skillet, heat the oil over high heat until hot but not smoking. Add the turkey cutlets (reserving any salsa in bowl) and onions. Adjust the heat so the cutlets cook rapidly but do not burn. Cook, turning the cutlets several times, until they are nicely colored and just cooked through, about 5 minutes. Return the cutlets to the bowl with the reserved salsa.

3 Add the green chiles, corn, bean, and pepper mixture, cilantro (or parsley), and remaining 1/4 cup salsa to the skillet. Cook, stirring occasionally, about 5 minutes longer, until the flavors are well blended.

4 Return the cutlets to the skillet, along with the reserved salsa. Continue simmering, about 5 minutes longer, until the cutlets and corn mixture are heated to piping hot. Add salt and pepper to taste. Garnish with additional cilantro (or parsley), if desired.

Turkey Cutlet Skillet Dijonnaise

"A package of ready-to-use turkey breast cutlets and a little Dijon mustard are the keys to this tempting but remarkably simple skillet meal."

1 1/2 cups coarsely sliced baby carrots

About 1 cup fat-free low-sodium or regular chicken broth

1 Tbsp olive oil

4 4-oz turkey breast cutlets

2 Tbsp Dijon mustard

1/8 tsp black pepper, or to taste

2 1/4 cups small cauliflower or broccoli florets, or a combination of the two

PREP TIME: 15 MINUTES

SERVINGS: 4

SERVING SIZE: 4-OZ CUTLET, PLUS 3/4 CUP VEGETABLE MIXTURE

Exchanges
4 Very Lean Meat
2 Vegetable

Calories 192
    Calories from Fat 38
Total Fat . . . . .4 g
    Saturated Fat . . . . .1 g
Cholesterol . . . . .73 mg
Sodium . . . . .378 mg
Total Carbohydrate . . . . .8 g
    Dietary Fiber . . . . .3 g
    Sugars . . . . .5 g
Protein . . . . .30 g

1 In a 12-inch nonstick skillet over medium-high heat, combine the carrots and 3/4 cup broth. Bring to a boil and cook until the carrots are almost tender and most of the broth has evaporated from the skillet, about 5 minutes.

2 Push the carrots to the side, and add the oil and turkey cutlets to the skillet. Using a table knife, smooth half the mustard over one side of the cutlets. Turn over the cutlets and smooth the remaining mustard over them. Sprinkle lightly with the pepper. Add the cauliflower (or broccoli) to the skillet around the cutlets.

3 Adjust the heat so the cutlets simmer. Cook, stirring the vegetables and turning the cutlets several times, until the cutlets are very lightly browned and just cooked through when checked in the thickest part with a paring knife, about 5 or 6 minutes. If the skillet begins to boil dry, add a few tablespoons of chicken broth as needed.

TEX-MEX GROUND BEEF SKILLET

If you're a fan of Tex-Mex fare, you'll love the pleasing combination of flavors and textures in this quick skillet dinner.

3/4 lb extra lean ground beef

1 medium green bell pepper, seeded and diced

1 large celery stalk, sliced

1/2 cup mild salsa

1 cup chopped fresh tomato, drained

3/4 cup water

1 cup frozen corn kernels

1 cup canned chickpeas, washed and drained

1 1/2 tsp chili powder

1/4 tsp salt

1/2 cup uncooked quick-cooking rice

3/4 cup shredded fat-free cheddar cheese

1 In a large nonstick skillet, cook the beef, green pepper, and celery over medium heat, stirring frequently, until the beef is browned, about 6 to 8 minutes.

2 Add salsa, tomato, water, corn, chickpeas, chili powder, and salt. Cover and bring to a boil. Reduce the heat, and simmer 10 to 12 minutes stirring occasionally.

3 Bring to a boil. Add the rice, and stir into the sauce. Cover, remove pan from heat, and allow to sit until the rice is tender, about 5 minutes. Sprinkle on cheese and stir into mixture.

PREP TIME: 10 MINUTES

SERVINGS: 4

SERVING SIZE: 1 1/2 CUPS

Exchanges
2 1/2 Starch
2 Vegetable
3 Lean Meat

Calories 353
    Calories from Fat 45
Total Fat . . . . .5 g
    Saturated Fat . . . . .1 g
Cholesterol . . . . .49 mg
Sodium . . . . .621 mg
Total Carbohydrate . . . .47 g
    Dietary Fiber . . . . .6 g
    Sugars . . . . .4 g
Protein . . . . .30 g

HAM AND VEGETABLE SKILLET

Quick and easy, this dinner goes from skillet to table in a snap.

2 cups frozen pepper and onion stir-fry medley

3/4 lb fully cooked 95 percent fat-free ham slice, cut into bite-sized pieces

1 Tbsp olive oil

2 cups frozen green beans

1 15-oz can chunky Italian-style tomato sauce

4 oz uncooked angel hair pasta

PREP TIME: 10 MINUTES

SERVINGS: 4

SERVING SIZE: 1 CUP, PLUS 1 OZ PASTA

Exchanges
1 1/2 Starch
4 Vegetable
1 Lean Meat
1/2 Fat

Calories . . . . .305 g
   Calories from Fat 65
Total Fat . . . . .7 g
   Saturated Fat . . . . . . .2 g
Cholesterol . . . . .37 mg
Sodium . . . . .1663 mg
Total Carbohydrate . . . .42 g
   Dietary Fiber . . . . . . .5 g
   Sugars . . . . .18 g
Protein . . . . .20 g

1 Cut up any large onion chunks in the pepper-onion mixture. In a large nonstick skillet, combine the peppers and onions, ham, and oil. Cook over medium heat, stirring frequently, until the onion has softened, about 5 or 6 minutes.

2 Add the green beans and tomato sauce. Bring to a boil. Reduce heat, cover, and simmer 8 or 9 minutes or until the green beans are cooked.

3 Meanwhile, cook the pasta according to package directions. Serve the ham and vegetables over the pasta.

MEXICAN-STYLE GROUND BEEF HASH

This is a full-flavored, slightly spicy beef hash inspired by a tangy Mexican dish called picadillo. Often used as a condiment or filling, picadillo frequently features the interesting sweet-tart-salty taste of apples and raisins, tomatoes, vinegar, and green olives, along with the meat. Here, we combine typical picadillo flavors to create a lively, colorful ground beef hash.

2/3 lb extra-lean ground beef

2 medium celery ribs, chopped

1 large onion, chopped

1/2 cup tomato ketchup or chili sauce

Scant 1/2 tsp ground cinnamon

1/8 tsp salt (optional)

1 cup diced canned no-salt-added tomatoes, including juice, or regular diced canned tomatoes

1 4-oz can chopped mild green chiles

1 medium Golden Delicious or other sweet, flavorful apple, chopped (unpeeled)

1/4 cup dark or golden raisins

2 Tbsp chopped pimiento-stuffed olives

2 cups diced cooked potatoes (or 2 cups cooked brown or white rice)

PREP TIME: 15 MINUTES

SERVINGS: 4

SERVING SIZE: 1 1/2 CUPS

Exchanges
2 Starch
1/2 Fruit
2 Vegetable
2 Very Lean Meat

Calories 300
    Calories from Fat 36
Total Fat . . . . .4 g
    Saturated Fat . . . . .1 g
Cholesterol . . . . .40 mg
Sodium . . . . .669 mg
Total Carbohydrate . . . .47 g
    Dietary Fiber . . . . .7 g
    Sugars . . . . .17 g
Protein . . . . .19 g

1 Combine the beef, celery, and onion in a 12-inch nonstick skillet over medium-high heat. Cook, stirring, until the beef is just cooked through, 5 to 6 minutes.

2 Stir in the ketchup, cinnamon, optional salt, tomatoes, green chiles, apples, raisins, and olives. Adjust the heat so the hash boils gently, and cook, stirring occasionally, about 8 to 10 minutes until the flavors are well blended.

3 Stir in the cooked potatoes (or rice). Heat until piping hot and serve.

Handy Tip

If you don't happen to have any diced leftover cooked potato, it's easy to ready some by "baking" several well-scrubbed red bliss (or other thin-skinned) potatoes in a microwave oven. Simply puncture each potato all the way through with a skewer or thin-bladed knife. Then, place on a microwave-safe dish, cover loosely with wax paper, and microwave on high power for 5 to 7 minutes or until tender when poked with a skewer in the thickest part.

Pork Chops with Sweet Potatoes and Mandarin Oranges

"Though very quick and easy, this makes a delicious, colorful, and wholesome meal."

2 tsp olive oil

4 4-oz well-trimmed boneless loin
   pork chops

1/8 to 1/4 tsp salt for seasoning chops

4 or 5 green onions, including tender green
   tops, cut into 1/2-inch lengths

1 10-oz can mandarin oranges (packed in
   juice), including juice

2 Tbsp lite soy sauce

1 large sweet potato (about 10 oz), peeled
   and cut into 1/3-inch cubes

Black pepper to taste (optional)

PREP TIME: 15 MINUTES

SERVINGS: 4

SERVING SIZE: 1 PORK CHOP,
   PLUS 3/4 CUP VEGETABLE
   ORANGE MIXTURE

Exchanges
1 Starch
1/2 Fruit
3 Lean Meat

Calories 277
   Calories from Fat 83
Total Fat . . . . .9 g
   Saturated Fat . . . . . . .3 g
Cholesterol . . . . .71 mg
Sodium . . . . .437 mg
Total Carbohydrate . . . .22 g
   Dietary Fiber . . . . . . .3 g
   Sugars . . . . .13 g
Protein . . . . .27 g

1 In a 12-inch nonstick skillet, heat the oil over medium-high heat. Add the pork chops and sprinkle both sides with salt. Cook the chops, turning occasionally, until nicely browned on both sides, about 7 minutes.

2 Add green onions and continue cooking until they are limp, about 2 minutes.

3 Add the juice from the oranges to the skillet; reserve the orange segments. Stir in the soy sauce, sweet potato cubes, and pepper. Adjust the heat so the liquid simmers gently and cook 8 to 10 minutes longer, or until the sweet potato is just tender when tested with a fork. The liquid should cook down to only a tablespoon or so; if the pan begins to boil dry, stir in a few teaspoons of water.

4 Gently stir the orange segments into the skillet. Continue cooking just until they are piping hot.

PORK CHOPS AND VEGETABLES A LA MEXICANA

A package of pork chops and a frozen vegetable medley of corn, celery, bell peppers, and black beans make it easy to turn out this colorful Tex-Mex style skillet quickly. (If this particular vegetable combo isn't available where you shop, simply substitute a similar one, such as corn, lima beans, and sweet peppers.)

1 Tbsp olive oil

4 4-oz boneless loin pork chops, trimmed of excess fat

1/2 tsp mild to medium-hot chili powder

1/2 tsp dried thyme leaves

1/4 tsp salt

1 8-oz can no-added-salt or regular tomato sauce

1/4 cup mild or medium-hot salsa or picante sauce

1 14-oz package frozen (thawed) corn, celery, bell pepper, and black bean medley or another similar frozen vegetable medley

PREP TIME: 15 MINUTES

SERVINGS: 4

SERVING SIZE: 1 PORK CHOP, PLUS 3/4 CUP VEGETABLE MIXTURE

Exchanges
1/2 Starch
1 Vegetable
4 Lean Meat

Calories 308
   Calories from Fat 92
Total Fat . . . . .10 g
   Saturated Fat . . . . .3 g
Cholesterol . . . . .71 mg
Sodium . . . . .318 mg
Total Carbohydrate . . . .16 g
   Dietary Fiber . . . . .7 g
   Sugars . . . . .6 g
Protein . . . . .30 g

1 Heat the oil in a 12-inch nonstick skillet over medium-high heat. Add the pork chops and sprinkle on one side with half the chili powder, thyme, and salt. Turn over and sprinkle the remaining seasonings on the second side.

2 Cook the chops, turning occasionally, until well browned on both sides, 6 or 7 minutes.

3 Lower the heat slightly. Stir 1/3 cup water, then the tomato sauce and salsa into the skillet. Turn the chops to coat with the sauce. Adjust the heat so the sauce simmers gently, and cook 8 minutes longer. If the pan begins to boil dry, stir in a few teaspoons water as needed.

4 Stir the vegetables into the pan and continue cooking until the vegetables and chops are just cooked through, 5 to 7 minutes longer; if necessary, stir in a little water to keep the pan from boiling dry. Taste and add more salt, if desired.

POTATO-CABBAGE SKILLET WITH SAUSAGE

This extra-good and easy recipe takes advantage of the pre-cooked, lower-fat turkey sausage that's available today. Read labels and look for brands that have no more than 7 1/2 grams of fat for a 3-oz portion of sausage or 5 grams of fat for a 2-oz portion.

2 1/4 cups fat-free low-sodium or regular chicken broth

1/8 tsp black pepper, or to taste

2 medium red bliss or other thin-skinned boiling potatoes, very thinly sliced

1 cup frozen (thawed) cut green beans

2 or 3 green onions, including tender tops, coarsely chopped

6 cups very coarsely sliced green cabbage

3/4 lb lower-fat smoked turkey Kielbasa sausage or similar sausage in casings, cut crosswise into 1/4-inch slices

PREP TIME: 15 MINUTES

SERVINGS: 4

SERVING SIZE: 1 1/2 CUPS VEGETABLES & SAUSAGE

Exchanges
1 Starch
2 Vegetable
2 Lean Meat

Calories 245
    Calories from Fat 71
Total Fat . . . . .8 g
    Saturated Fat . . . . .2 g
Cholesterol . . . . .54 mg
Sodium . . . . .1574 mg
Total Carbohydrate . . . .25 g
    Dietary Fiber . . . . .5 g
    Sugars . . . . .9 g
Protein . . . . .18 g

1 In a 12-inch or similar nonstick skillet over medium-high heat, combine the broth and pepper and bring to a boil.

2 Add the potato slices and green beans and boil, uncovered and stirring occasionally, for 6 to 8 minutes, or until the slices are barely cooked through when tested with a fork. If the skillet begins to boil dry, add a little water.

3 Sprinkle the green onions, then the cabbage, over the potatoes. Top with the sausage slices. Reduce the heat so the pan simmers gently. Cover tightly and cook 4 to 6 minutes or until cabbage is just tender when tested with a fork. Stir to combine ingredients, then spoon into soup plates.

TANGY BEANS AND BACON

"The smoky taste of Canadian bacon permeates this skillet dinner. Check cans of Italian-seasoned tomato sauce, because some have more sugar than others. You want a lower-sugar brand."

1 large onion, chopped

1 large celery stalk, diced

1 Tbsp olive oil

2/3 cup defatted beef broth, divided

1 15-oz can Italian-seasoned tomato sauce

1 6-oz Canadian bacon, cut into narrow strips

1 19-oz can white kidney beans (cannelloni), rinsed and drained

1 red bell pepper, seeded and diced (if unavailable, use green bell pepper)

1/4 tsp black pepper or to taste

1 In a large nonstick skillet, combine the onion and celery with the oil and 2 tablespoons of the broth. Cook, stirring, over medium heat, about 6 or 7 minutes or until the celery is almost tender. If the liquid begins to evaporate, add a bit more broth.

2 Add the tomato sauce, remaining broth, bacon, beans, red bell pepper, and black pepper. Stir to mix well. Bring to a boil. Reduce the heat, cover, and simmer 10 to 12 minutes. Serve in bowls.

PREP TIME: 15 MINUTES

SERVINGS: 4

SERVING SIZE: 1 CUP

Exchanges
1 1/2 Starch
3 Vegetable
1/2 Fat
1 Lean Meat

Calories 269
   Calories from Fat 60
Total Fat . . . . .7 g
   Saturated Fat . . . . .2 g
Cholesterol . . . . .20 mg
Sodium . . . . .1383 mg
Total Carbohydrate . . . .36 g
   Dietary Fiber . . . . . . .10 g
   Sugars . . . . .7 g
Protein . . . . .19 g

SHRIMP AND OLIVES WITH TOMATO-FETA SAUCE

The feta and olives blend to give this quick and easy skillet a wonderful flavor.

2 Tbsp olive oil

1 medium onion, chopped

1 cup sliced zucchini

1 15-oz can chunky Italian-style tomato sauce

6 large green pimiento olives, sliced

1 lb ready-to-cook shrimp

1/2 cup crumbled feta cheese

5 oz (about 1 1/2 cups) penne or other similar pasta, cooked according to package directions

1 In a large nonstick skillet, combine the oil, onion, and zucchini. Cook over medium heat, stirring frequently, until the onion has softened, about 5 to 6 minutes.

2 Stir in the tomato sauce and olives, and simmer for 2 or 3 minutes. Stir in shrimp, and cook an additional minute. Stir in cheese, and simmer an additional 1 or 2 minutes.

3 Serve over pasta.

PREP TIME: 12 MINUTES

SERVINGS: 5

SERVING SIZE: 1 CUP, PLUS 1 OZ PASTA

Exchanges
1 1/2 Starch
2 Vegetable
1/2 Fat
2 Lean Meat

Calories 307
    Calories from Fat 95
Total Fat . . . . .11 g
    Saturated Fat . . . . .3 g
Cholesterol . . . . .116 mg
Sodium . . . . .885 mg
Total Carbohydrate . . . .31 g
    Dietary Fiber . . . . .3 g
    Sugars . . . . .9 g
Protein . . . . .22 g

BROCCOLI FETA OMELETTE

We used to think that making omelettes was difficult, until we came across this easy method. This omelette makes a nice brunch or luncheon entree.

1 Tbsp olive oil

2 cups chopped broccoli florets

1/4 cup chopped onion

1 1/2 cups liquid egg substitute

1/2 tsp dried dill weed

Salt to taste (optional)

1/8 tsp pepper

1/2 cup reduced-fat finely crumbled feta cheese

4 whole-wheat luncheon rolls (optional)

PREP TIME: 10 MINUTES

SERVINGS: 4

SERVING SIZE: 1/4 OF OMELETTE

Exchanges
2 Starch
1 Fat
1 Medium-Fat Meat

Calories 180
    Calories from Fat 72
Total Fat . . . . .8 g
    Saturated Fat . . . . . . .2 g
Cholesterol . . . . .6 mg
Sodium . . . . .383 mg
Total Carbohydrate . . . . .9 g
    Dietary Fiber . . . . . . .4 g
    Sugars . . . . .1 g
Protein . . . . .18 g

1 In a large nonstick skillet with sloping sides, combine the oil, broccoli, and onion. Cook over medium heat, stirring frequently, until the onion is tender, about 5 or 6 minutes.

2 Meanwhile, place the egg substitute in a medium bowl. With a fork, beat in the dill, salt, if desired, and pepper.

3 When the onion is tender, add the egg substitute to the pan, tipping the pan so that the egg mixture covers the entire bottom. Cook over medium heat for 2 minutes. Sprinkle the cheese over the top of the egg mixture. Cover, reduce heat, and cook an additional 4 to 6 minutes or until the omelette is set.

4 With a plastic spatula, cut the omelette into four servings, and transfer the servings to plates. Serve with luncheon rolls, if desired.

PASTA WITH TOMATO-FETA SAUCE

Here's a quick and delicious meatless pasta dinner.

> 1 Tbsp olive oil
>
> 1 medium onion, chopped
>
> 2 cups sliced zucchini
>
> 2 14 1/2-oz cans chunky Italian-style tomato sauce
>
> 8 to 10 Kalamata olives, pitted and cut into small pieces
>
> 1/2 cup crumbled feta cheese
>
> 5 oz spaghetti, cooked according to package directions

1 In a large skillet, combine the oil, onion, and zucchini. Cook over medium heat, stirring frequently, until the onion has softened, about 5 to 6 minutes.

2 Stir in the tomato sauce and olives, and simmer for 2 or 3 minutes. Stir in the cheese, and simmer an additional 1 or 2 minutes.

3 Serve over pasta.

PREP TIME: 12 MINUTES

SERVINGS: 5

SERVING SIZE: 1 CUP, PLUS 1 OZ PASTA

Exchanges
1 1/2 Starch
3 Vegetable
1 Fat

Calories 243
  Calories from Fat 65
Total Fat . . . . .7 g
  Saturated Fat . . . . .3 g
Cholesterol . . . . .13 mg
Sodium . . . . .1222 mg
Total Carbohydrate . . . .38 g
  Dietary Fiber . . . . .4 g
  Sugars . . . . .12 g
Protein . . . . .9 g

HEARTY SOUPS

CHICKEN MINESTRONE

"Colorful and savory, this makes a fine meal-in-a-bowl. The yield is large, so you may want to freeze part of the recipe for later use."

1 1/2 Tbsp olive oil

1 lb skinless, bone-in chicken breast halves

1 large onion, chopped

1 large celery stalk, cut crosswise into 1/4-inch pieces

2 medium carrots, cut crosswise into 1/8-inch slices

1 cup coarsely diced green or red bell pepper

4 1/2 cups fat-free low-sodium or regular chicken broth

1 cup hot water

1 cup coarsely cubed red bliss or other thin-skinned boiling potatoes

1 tsp dried oregano leaves

1/3 cup small macaroni (uncooked)

1 medium zucchini, coarsely diced

1 cup cannellini beans or great northern white beans, rinsed and well drained

1 14 1/2-oz can diced canned tomatoes (seasoned with garlic and onion)

Salt and black pepper to taste (optional)

PREP TIME: 30 MINUTES

SERVINGS: 12

SERVING SIZE: 1 CUP

Exchanges
1/2 Starch
1 Vegetable
1 Very Lean Meat
1/2 Fat

Calories 128
    Calories from Fat 23
Total Fat . . . . .3 g
    Saturated Fat . . . . .1 g
Cholesterol . . . . .18 mg
Sodium . . . . .399 mg
Total Carbohydrate . . . .15 g
    Dietary Fiber . . . . .3 g
    Sugars . . . . .5 g
Protein . . . . .11 g

1 In a very large saucepan or soup pot, combine the oil and chicken pieces over high heat. Lightly brown the chicken on all sides. Add the onion, celery, carrot, and bell pepper, and cook, stirring occasionally, until the onion is translucent, about 3 minutes longer.

2 Add the broth, 1 cup hot water, the potatoes, and oregano. Bring to a gentle boil over medium-high heat; cook for 15 minutes. Remove the chicken; set aside to cool.

3 Raise the heat to high and bring the mixture to a full boil. Stir in the macaroni and zucchini; boil, stirring occasionally, for 5 minutes. Add the beans; reduce the heat slightly and simmer 5 minutes longer, or until the pasta is just cooked through.

4 Meanwhile, remove the chicken meat from the bones. Cut into bite-sized pieces, then return to the pot, along with the tomatoes. Cook until heated through. Add salt and pepper to taste, if desired.

TORTILLA SOUP

This traditional Mexican soup is healthier when you use low-fat tortilla chips and nutritious veggies.

1 lb ground beef round

1 medium onion, chopped

4 cups fat-free low-sodium or regular chicken broth

1 15-oz can Mexican-flavored tomato sauce

1 can (16 oz) no-sodium-added kidney beans or regular kidney beans, well drained

2 cups frozen corn, broccoli, and red pepper mixture

Hot pepper sauce (optional)

Salt and pepper, to taste (optional)

2 1/2 cups coarsely crushed baked tortilla chips

PREP TIME: 15 MINUTES

SERVINGS: 10

SERVING SIZE: 1 CUP

Exchanges
1 Starch
1 Lean Meat
2 Vegetable

Calories 189
    Calories from Fat 20
Total Fat . . . . .2 g
    Saturated Fat . . . . .0 g
Cholesterol . . . . .23 mg
Sodium . . . . .589 mg
Total Carbohydrate . . . .27 g
    Dietary Fiber . . . . .4 g
    Sugars . . . . .7 g
Protein . . . . .16 g

1 In a Dutch oven or similar large, heavy pot, combine the ground round and onion. Cook over medium heat, stirring frequently, until the meat has browned, about 5 or 6 minutes.

2 Skim off and discard any excess fat.

3 Add the chicken broth, tomato sauce, beans, and mixed vegetables.

4 Stir to mix well. Bring to a boil. Cover, reduce the heat, and simmer 20 minutes. Add hot sauce if desired. Add salt and pepper if desired.

5 Ladle soup into bowls. Garnish each serving with 1/4 cup crushed tortilla chips.

CURRIED LENTIL-VEGETABLE SOUP WITH HAM

This recipe calls for red lentils, which are smaller and cook faster than the more common pale green or brown lentils. You can substitute green or brown lentils, if necessary, but they will require 30 to 40 minutes to become tender. In this case, very coarsely dice the potatoes to prevent them from overcooking.

1 Tbsp olive oil

1 large onion, chopped

1 large carrot, chopped

6 cups fat-free low-sodium or regular chicken broth

1 1/2 cups diced red bliss or other thin-skinned boiling potatoes

2/3 cup diced lean smoked ham

1/4 cup red lentils

1 1/2 Tbsp mild or hot curry powder

1 tsp dried thyme leaves

1/4 tsp caraway or fennel seeds

1 1/2 cups loose-packed frozen spinach, thawed, coarse stems removed, and chopped (or 2 cups fresh spinach leaves, well washed, coarse stems removed, and chopped)

1/2 cup bottled roasted red sweet peppers, drained and chopped

Salt and black pepper to taste (optional)

PREP TIME: 25 MINUTES

SERVINGS: 6

SERVING SIZE: 1 CUP

Exchanges
1 Starch
1 Vegetable
1 Lean Meat

Calories 144
   Calories from Fat 31
Total Fat . . . . .3 g
   Saturated Fat . . . . .1 g
Cholesterol . . . . .9 mg
Sodium . . . . .745 mg
Total Carbohydrate . . . .18 g
   Dietary Fiber . . . . .4 g
   Sugars . . . . .6 g
Protein . . . . .11 g

1 In a very large saucepan or large pot over medium-high heat, combine the oil, onions, and carrots. Cook, stirring, until onions are lightly browned, about 5 minutes.

2 Add the broth, potatoes, ham, lentils, curry powder, thyme leaves, and caraway seeds. Bring the mixture to a boil, stirring occasionally. Lower the heat, cover the pot, and simmer the mixture, stirring occasionally, for 18 to 20 minutes, or until the lentils are just tender.

3 Stir in the spinach and roasted peppers and simmer 3 or 4 minutes longer, until the spinach is tender.

4 Add salt and pepper, if desired.

HAM AND BEAN SOUP

" We love bean soups. This one's ready in a snap because it's made with canned beans. You can make it with leftover ham or with part of a purchased ham slice. "

1 large onion, chopped

3 large celery stalks, minced

1 tsp minced garlic

1 Tbsp olive oil

3 cups fat-free low-sodium or regular chicken broth, divided

1 19-oz can cannellini beans, rinsed and well drained

1 15-oz can chunky Italian-style tomato sauce

1/2 lb low-fat ham, cut into small pieces

3/4 oz uncooked angel hair pasta, broken into 2-inch pieces (about 1/3 cup)

Salt to taste (optional)

PREP TIME: 20 MINUTES

SERVINGS: 7

SERVING SIZE: 1 CUP

Exchanges
1 Starch
1 Lean Meat
2 Vegetable

Calories 171
    Calories from Fat 31
Total Fat . . . . .3 g
    Saturated Fat . . . . . . .1 g
Cholesterol . . . . .16 mg
Sodium . . . . .1045 mg
Total Carbohydrate . . . .24 g
    Dietary Fiber . . . . .5 g
    Sugars . . . . .7 g
Protein . . . . .13 g

1 In a small Dutch oven or similar pot, combine the onion, celery, garlic, oil, and 1/4 cup broth. Cook over medium-high heat, stirring frequently, 6 or 7 minutes, or until the onion is tender.

2 Add the remaining broth, beans, tomato sauce, and ham. Bring to a boil over high heat. Reduce the heat and simmer, uncovered, stirring occasionally, 15 minutes.

3 Bring the soup to a boil. Stir in the pasta. Reduce the heat, and cook at a low boil 4 or 5 minutes until the pasta is tender. Add salt, if desired.

POTATO-KALE SOUP WITH HAM

This easy recipe is inspired by a traditional Portuguese soup that features potato and kale. Even those who aren't fans of this very healthful green vegetable often enjoy the soup.

4 to 5 *oz fresh untrimmed kale leaves (enough to yield 4 lightly packed cups torn leaves)*

1 *large onion, chopped*

2 *medium celery stalks, chopped*

1 1/2 *Tbsp olive oil*

4 *cups fat-free low-sodium or regular chicken broth*

2 1/2 *cups cubed (1/3-inch) red bliss or other thin-skinned boiling potatoes*

1 *tsp dried marjoram leaves*

1/2 *tsp dried thyme leaves*

1/4 *tsp black pepper*

1/2 *cup lean, well-trimmed diced smoked ham*

PREP TIME: 20 MINUTES

SERVINGS: 6

SERVING SIZE: 1 CUP

Exchanges
1 Starch
1 Vegetable
1/2 Fat

Calories 131
   Calories from Fat 35
Total Fat . . . . .4 g
   Saturated Fat . . . . .1 g
Cholesterol . . . . .7 mg
Sodium . . . . .498 mg
Total Carbohydrate . . . .17 g
   Dietary Fiber . . . . .3 g
   Sugars . . . . .5 g
Protein . . . . .7 g

1 Thoroughly rinse the kale in a colander under running water. Tear the leafy parts from the ribs into 2-inch pieces, discarding the ribs and stems as you work. Measure out enough to yield 4 lightly packed cups. Rinse the leaves again. Put the leaves in a large bowl of water, swishing them around. Let stand so any loosened grit can sink to the bottom. Scoop up the leaves with your hands and return them to the colander. Rinse once more; let stand to drain.

2 In a 3- to 4-quart saucepan or soup pot, combine the onion, celery, and oil. Cook over medium-high heat, stirring frequently, 3 or 4 minutes, until the onion is soft.

3 Stir in the broth, potatoes, kale, marjoram, thyme, and pepper. Bring to a boil over high heat. Reduce the heat; simmer, uncovered, stirring occasionally, for 6 minutes.

4 Stir the ham into the pot. Cover and simmer until the potatoes and kale are tender, 6 to 10 minutes longer. Thin the soup with a little water, if desired.

EASY MEDITERRANEAN FISH SOUP

Served along with crusty bread, this robust, stew-like soup makes a good, healthful, hurry-up meal. Note that the recipe calls for saffron, an unusual—and pricey!—spice that is an essential ingredient in the dish. (The good news is that a little saffron goes a long way.) Traditionally, the soup also includes fennel seeds, but you can substitute caraway seeds if that's what you have on hand.

1/8 tsp finely crumbled saffron threads combined with 1/2 cup hot water

2 Tbsp olive oil

1 medium onion, chopped

1 large celery stalk, chopped

1/2 cup diced red or green bell pepper, or a combination

1 large clove garlic, peeled and minced

2 14 1/2-oz cans diced tomatoes, including juice

2 Tbsp dry sherry, dry marsala wine, or orange juice

1/4 tsp black pepper, or to taste

1/8 tsp fennel seeds, or a pinch of caraway seeds

1 lb fresh or frozen boneless, skinless flounder or other mild white-fleshed fish, cut into 3/4-inch chunks

1/8 tsp salt (optional)

PREP TIME: 20 MINUTES

SERVINGS: 4

SERVING SIZE: 1 1/4 CUPS

Exchanges
3 Very Lean Meat
1 Fat
3 Vegetable

Calories 222
   Calories from Fat 71
Total Fat . . . . .8 g
   Saturated Fat . . . . .2 g
Cholesterol . . . . .54 mg
Sodium . . . . .515 mg
Total Carbohydrate . . . .14 g
   Dietary Fiber . . . . .4 g
   Sugars . . . . .10 g
Protein . . . . .24 g

1 Set the saffron-water mixture aside while the remaining ingredients are readied.

2 In a 2 1/2- to 3-quart pot or saucepan, heat the oil to hot but not smoking over high heat. Add the onion, celery, bell pepper, and garlic. Lower the heat to medium-high, and cook, stirring, until the vegetables are well browned, about 5 or 6 minutes.

3 Stir the tomatoes, sherry, black pepper, and fennel seeds (or caraway seeds) into the pot. Add the saffron-water mixture. Reduce the heat so the mixture simmers gently. Simmer, covered, stirring occasionally, for 20 minutes.

4 Stir in the fish pieces. Simmer about 2 to 3 minutes longer until the fish pieces are just cooked through and flavors are well blended. Taste and stir in salt, if desired. If the soup seems too thick, thin it with a little hot water.

Manhattan-Style Clam Chowder

Here's a super-quick clam chowder. We leave the potato unpeeled for ease of preparation, but you can peel it if you like.

2 1/4 cups fat-free low-sodium or regular
    chicken broth

1 large red bliss potato, diced

2 cups mixed frozen bell pepper and
    onion stir-fry

3 6 1/2-oz cans chopped clams,
    including juice

1 14 1/2-oz can low-sodium or regular
    diced tomatoes

1 8-oz can low-sodium or regular
    tomato sauce

1 cup frozen corn

1 bay leaf

1 tsp dried thyme leaves

1/2 tsp dried marjoram leaves

    Salt and pepper to taste (optional)

PREP TIME: 15 MINUTES

SERVINGS: 9

SERVING SIZE: 1 CUP

Exchanges
1/2 Starch
1 Very Lean Meat
1 Vegetable

Calories 96
   Calories from Fat 8
Total Fat . . . . .1 g
   Saturated Fat . . . . .0 g
Cholesterol . . . . .20 mg
Sodium . . . . .241 mg
Total Carbohydrate . . . .13 g
   Dietary Fiber . . . . . . .2 g
   Sugars . . . . .5 g
Protein . . . . .10 g

1 In a large heavy saucepan or Dutch oven, combine the broth, potato, and pepper and onion mixture. Bring to a boil. Cover, reduce the heat, and cook 8 to 10 minutes until the potato is almost tender.

2 Add the clams and their liquid. Add the tomatoes, tomato sauce, corn, bay leaf, thyme, and marjoram. Recover and bring to a boil.

3 Lower the heat and simmer about 15 minutes longer, until the flavors are well blended. Remove and discard the bay leaf. Add salt and pepper to taste, if desired.

Corn, Potato, and Clam Chowder

Traditional New England clam chowders always pair potatoes with clams, but as this recipe proves, corn is also a very appealing addition to clam chowder.

1 medium onion, chopped

1 large celery stalk, chopped

1 Tbsp olive oil

2 cups fat-free low-sodium or regular chicken broth

2 3/4 cups peeled and cubed (1/3-inch) boiling potatoes

1 tsp dried marjoram leaves

1/2 tsp dried basil leaves

1/2 cup reduced-fat milk

2 1/2 cups frozen (thawed) corn kernels

2 10 1/2-oz cans minced clams, including broth

Salt and black pepper to taste (optional)

PREP TIME: 20 MINUTES

SERVINGS: 8

SERVING SIZE: 1 CUP

Exchanges
1 1/2 Starch
1 Very Lean Meat

Calories 168
  Calories from Fat 26
Total Fat . . . . .3 g
  Saturated Fat . . . . .1 g
Cholesterol . . . . .25 mg
Sodium . . . . .266 mg
Total Carbohydrate . . . .24 g
  Dietary Fiber . . . . .3 g
  Sugars . . . . .6 g
Protein . . . . .13 g

1 In a very large saucepan or soup pot, combine the onion, celery, and oil. Cook over medium-high heat, stirring frequently, 3 or 4 minutes, until the onion is soft.

2 Add the broth, potatoes, marjoram, and basil. Bring to a boil over high heat. Reduce the heat and simmer, uncovered, stirring occasionally, until the potatoes are barely tender, 10 to 12 minutes.

3 Scoop up 2 cups vegetables from the pan. Combine with the milk in a blender or food processor. Blend or process until the mixture is completely pureed and smooth. Return the pureed mixture to the saucepan.

4 Stir the corn and clams into the saucepan. Return to a simmer; cook 5 to 8 minutes longer, until the flavors have blended. Add salt and pepper to taste, if desired.

CREOLE-STYLE FISH SOUP

"This easy soup has real New Orleans flavor."

1 cup chopped onion

1 tsp minced garlic

2 Tbsp olive oil

3 cups fat-free low-sodium or regular chicken broth

1 14 1/2-oz can low-sodium diced tomatoes

2 cups frozen mixed corn, broccoli, and red pepper

1/2 tsp dried basil leaves

1 tsp dried thyme leaves

1/2 tsp dried marjoram leaves

1/8 tsp black pepper

3 to 4 drops hot pepper sauce, or to taste (optional)

1/4 tsp salt, or to taste (optional)

3/4 lb fresh or frozen (thawed) skinless fish filets such as perch, flounder, sole, halibut, or turbot, cut into large bite-sized pieces

1/2 cup quick-cooking rice

PREP TIME: 18 MINUTES

SERVINGS: 8

SERVING SIZE: 1 CUP

Exchanges
1/2 Starch
1 Vegetable
1 Very Lean Meat
1 Fat

Calories 141
  Calories from Fat 37
Total Fat . . . . .4 g
  Saturated Fat . . . . .1 g
Cholesterol . . . . .13 mg
Sodium . . . . .225 mg
Total Carbohydrate . . . .13 g
  Dietary Fiber . . . . .2 g
  Sugars . . . . .4 g
Protein . . . . .12 g

1 In a Dutch oven or similar large heavy pot, combine the onion, garlic, and oil. Cook over medium heat 6 to 7 minutes, stirring frequently, until the onion is tender.

2 Add the broth, tomatoes, and mixed vegetables. Add the basil, thyme, marjoram, black pepper, and hot pepper sauce, if desired. Stir to combine well. Bring to a boil. Cover, reduce heat, and simmer 10 to 15 minutes, until the vegetables are tender, stirring occasionally. Add salt, if desired.

3 Add fish and rice, and cook an additional 5 or 6 minutes until fish is cooked through.

FRESH SALMON CHOWDER

This is a mild, yet very appealing chowder.

3/4 *lb fresh, boneless salmon filet (skin intact), cut in half crosswise*

3 *cups fat-free low-sodium or regular chicken broth, divided*

1 *large onion, chopped*

2 *medium celery stalks, chopped*

1 *medium carrot, chopped*

1 *Tbsp olive oil*

1/2 *Tbsp tub-style corn oil margarine*

1 1/2 *Tbsp all-purpose white flour*

1 *cup reduced-fat milk*

3 1/2 *cups peeled and cubed (1/3-inch) boiling potatoes*

1/2 *Tbsp prepared mustard*

3 *Tbsp chopped fresh dill weed, plus 1 Tbsp for garnish*

1/2 *tsp dried thyme leaves*

Salt and black pepper to taste (optional)

PREP TIME: 20 MINUTES

SERVINGS: 6

SERVING SIZE: 1 CUP

Exchanges
1 1/2 Starch
2 Lean Meat
1 Vegetable

Calories 245
   Calories from Fat 71
Total Fat . . . . .8 g
   Saturated Fat . . . . . . .1 g
Cholesterol . . . . .38 mg
Sodium . . . . .331 mg
Total Carbohydrate . . . .26 g
   Dietary Fiber . . . . . . .3 g
   Sugars . . . . .7 g
Protein . . . . .17 g

1 Lay the salmon pieces, skin-side down, in a very large saucepan or similar-size pot. Add 1/2 cup chicken broth. Bring to a simmer over medium-high heat. Cover the pot with a tight-fitting lid. Adjust the heat so the pot simmers gently and cook about 5 minutes, or until the salmon pieces are opaque all the way through when cut into and checked in the thickest part. Turn out the fish and liquid into a bowl.

2 Wipe out the pan used. Add the onion, celery, carrot, oil, and margarine to the pan. Cook over medium-high heat, stirring frequently, until the onion is tender, about 5 minutes.

3 Vigorously stir in the flour; cook 1 minute, stirring constantly. Add the remaining broth, stirring and scraping the pan bottom, then the milk, potatoes, mustard, dill, and thyme. Bring to a boil over high heat. Reduce the heat and simmer, covered, stirring and scraping the pan bottom occasionally, until the potatoes are tender, 15 to 20 minutes.

4 Meanwhile, remove and discard the salmon skin. Using a fork, flake the flesh into bite-sized pieces.

5 Stir the salmon pieces and any cooking broth into the saucepan. Return to a simmer and cook, covered, about 4 minutes longer, until the flavors have blended. If desired, thin the chowder with a little water. Add salt and pepper to taste, if desired. Garnish the soup with 1 tablespoon fresh dill weed just before serving.

Handy Tip

For fuss-free preparation, ask the seafood department clerk to remove the small lateral line bones along the thicker end of the salmon filet. (Some fish departments routinely do this.) Otherwise, run your hand along the length of the fish about an inch below the upper edge to locate these bones. Either use a sharp paring knife and cut away the bones in a long, thin sliver, or simply pull out the bones using tweezers or small pliers.

CHEESE TORTELLONI SOUP
WITH ENDIVE

A ready-to-cook package of fresh cheese tortelloni and a head of curly endive are the stars in this savory, yet easy soup. Since different brands of tortelloni require widely varying cooking times, check the package directions before you begin. Then, stir the tortelloni into the pot during the 15-minute cooking period at the point that will give them enough time to cook through.

1 medium head curly endive (about
    12 oz untrimmed)

1 Tbsp olive oil

1 small onion, chopped

1 medium carrot, finely diced

1 small garlic clove, peeled and minced

4 cups fat-free low-sodium or regular
    chicken broth

1 tsp dried marjoram leaves

1/8 tsp black pepper, to taste

1 9- to 12-oz package cheese tortelloni

PREP TIME: 20 MINUTES

SERVINGS: 5

SERVING SIZE: 1 CUP

Exchanges
1 Starch
1 Vegetable
1 Medium-Fat Meat

Calories 180
    Calories from Fat 51
Total Fat . . . . .6 g
    Saturated Fat . . . . .1 g
Cholesterol . . . . .16 mg
Sodium . . . . .550 mg
Total Carbohydrate . . . .23 g
    Dietary Fiber . . . . .2 g
    Sugars . . . . .5 g
Protein . . . . .9 g

1 Trim off and discard the root end and any tough or dry outer leaves from the endive. Thoroughly rinse the endive in a colander under running water. Discard any tough stalk ends. Tear the leaves into small (1-inch) pieces. Thoroughly rinse the leaves again; let stand until well drained. Measure out enough leaves to yield at least 3 lightly packed cups and up to 3 1/2 lightly packed cups.

2 In a 3-quart pot or very large saucepan, heat the oil to hot but not smoking, over high heat. Add the onion and carrot. Lower the heat slightly, and cook, stirring, until the onion just begins to brown, about 3 minutes. Stir in the garlic and cook 1 minute longer.

3 Stir the broth, curly endive, marjoram, and pepper into the pot. (The endive will fill the pot at first, but will quickly cook down.) Bring to a boil over high heat.

4 Reduce the heat so the mixture simmers gently. Simmer, uncovered, stirring occasionally until the endive is tender, 12 to 15 minutes. Check the tortelloni cooking directions and add them into the pot at the point that will allow them to be cooked through when the endive is done. Before serving, thin the soup with a little hot water, if necessary. Serve in soup plates or bowls.

Broccoli-Cheddar Chowder

It's sometimes tricky to smoothly melt cheese into a soup. However, in this tasty recipe the cheese is quickly and easily incorporated using a blender or food processor.

1 large onion, chopped

1 large celery stalk, chopped

1 1/2 Tbsp olive oil

2 Tbsp all-purpose white flour

4 1/2 cups fat-free low-sodium or regular chicken broth

1 3/4 cups peeled and cubed (1/3-inch) boiling potatoes

1 1/2 tsp dried marjoram leaves

3 1/2 cups small broccoli florets

1/2 cup shredded reduced-fat sharp cheddar cheese

Salt and black pepper to taste (optional)

PREP TIME: 20 MINUTES

SERVINGS: 6

SERVING SIZE: 1 CUP

Exchanges
1 Starch
1 Vegetable
1 Fat

Calories 140
   Calories from Fat 48
Total Fat . . . . .5 g
   Saturated Fat . . . . .2 g
Cholesterol . . . . .7 mg
Sodium . . . . .424 mg
Total Carbohydrate . . . .17 g
   Dietary Fiber . . . . .3 g
   Sugars . . . . .5 g
Protein . . . . .7 g

1 In a large saucepan, combine the onion, celery, and oil. Cook over medium-high heat, stirring frequently, 3 or 4 minutes, until the onion is soft.

2 Stir in the flour until well combined. Stir in the broth, potatoes, and marjoram. Bring to a boil over high heat. Reduce the heat; simmer, uncovered, stirring occasionally, until the potatoes are barely tender, 12 to 14 minutes.

3 Scoop up 2 1/2 cups vegetables, then 1 cup broth from pan. Combine in a blender or food processor. Cool slightly. Blend or process until completely pureed and smooth. Return half the pureed mixture to the saucepan. Reserve the remainder of the puree in the blender or processor.

4 Stir the broccoli into the saucepan. Bring the mixture to a simmer. Cook 5 to 8 minutes longer, until the florets are just tender.

5 Sprinkle the cheddar over the reserved pureed vegetables; blend or process until well blended. Stir the cheese-vegetable mixture into the soup. Watching carefully, reheat to piping hot but not boiling. Add salt and pepper, if desired.

SPICY THREE-PEPPER SOUP WITH TOMATO AND CHEESE

Enlivened with green chiles, bell peppers, and jalapenos (the three peppers!), this soup is colorful and has a savory, south-of-the-border flavor. For best texture, use a blender.

2 medium onions, chopped

1 cup chopped red or green bell pepper (or a combination)

1 1/2 Tbsp olive oil

1 small clove garlic, peeled and minced

1 to 2 Tbsp seeded, finely chopped jalapeno (or to taste)

2 Tbsp all-purpose white flour

3 cups fat-free low-sodium or regular chicken broth

1 1/2 cups peeled and coarsely chopped (1/2-inch pieces) boiling potatoes

1/2 tsp dried thyme leaves

1/3 cup shredded reduced-fat sharp cheddar cheese

1 4- to 4 1/2-oz can chopped mild green chiles, drained

1 medium tomato, peeled, cored, and diced medium-fine

1/2 cup reduced-fat milk

Salt and black pepper to taste (optional)

PREP TIME: 20 MINUTES

SERVINGS: 6

SERVING SIZE: 1 CUP

Exchanges
1 Starch
1 Vegetable
1 Fat

Calories 143
   Calories from Fat 47
Total Fat . . . . .5 g
   Saturated Fat . . . . .2 g
Cholesterol . . . . .7 mg
Sodium . . . . .410 mg
Total Carbohydrate . . . .18 g
   Dietary Fiber . . . . .3 g
   Sugars . . . . .7 g
Protein . . . . .6 g

1 In a large saucepan, combine the onion, bell pepper, and oil. Cook over medium-high heat, stirring frequently, 4 to 6 minutes, until the onion is soft. Stir in the garlic and jalapeno; cook 30 seconds longer.

2 Stir in the flour until evenly incorporated. Stir in the broth, potatoes, and thyme. Bring to a boil over high heat. Reduce the heat; simmer, uncovered, stirring occasionally, until the potatoes are tender, 8 to 10 minutes.

3 Scoop up a generous 1 1/2 cups vegetables and 1 cup broth from the saucepan, placing them in a blender or food processor. Cool slightly. Then, add the cheese to the vegetables and broth. Blend or process until completely pureed and smooth; set aside.

4 Add the green chiles and chopped tomato. Bring the mixture to a simmer. Cook 5 to 7 minutes longer, until the tomato is just cooked through.

5 Return the cheese-vegetable mixture to the soup. Stir in the milk. Watching carefully, reheat to hot but not boiling. Add salt and pepper, if desired.

Handy Tips

Some jalapenos are much spicier than others, so start by carefully taking a small taste and then add them to the soup accordingly.

For a soup suitable for vegetarians, you can substitute vegetable broth for the chicken broth.

ITALIAN BREAD SOUP

Although it started out as hearty peasant fare, bread soup has migrated into trendy Italian restaurants. Traditionally, it's made with stale bread, but seasoned crouton stuffing mix works equally well.

1 1/2 cups chopped onion

2 tsp minced garlic

2 Tbsp olive oil

4 cups fat-free low-sodium or regular chicken broth

1 15-oz can Italian-seasoned tomato sauce

2 cups mixed frozen corn, red pepper, and broccoli

1 19-oz can cannellini beans, rinsed and drained

Pepper to taste

1 1/2 cups seasoned stuffing croutons

Scant 6 Tbsp grated Parmesan cheese

PREP TIME: **10** MINUTES

SERVINGS: **8**

SERVING SIZE: **1** CUP

Exchanges
1 1/2 Starch
2 Vegetable
1 Fat

Calories 217
   Calories from Fat 62
Total Fat . . . . .7 g
   Saturated Fat . . . . . . .2 g
Cholesterol . . . . .6 mg
Sodium . . . . .857 mg
Total Carbohydrate . . . .29 g
   Dietary Fiber . . . . . . .5 g
   Sugars . . . . .10 g
Protein . . . . .11 g

1 In a Dutch oven or similar large, heavy pot, combine the onion, garlic, and oil. Cook over medium heat, stirring frequently until the onion is tender, 5 to 6 minutes. If onions begin to stick, add some of the broth.

2 Add the remaining broth, tomato sauce, mixed vegetables, and beans. Bring to a boil. Cover, reduce heat, and simmer 20 minutes. Add pepper to taste.

3 To serve, arrange 3 tablespoons of bread cubes in each soup bowl. Ladle the soup over the cubes. Sprinkle each serving with about 2 teaspoons of Parmesan cheese.

TOMATO-SWEET POTATO BISQUE

This hearty, very savory vegetable bisque is quickly pureed in a food processor. It is enriched with a surprising, but tempting ingredient—peanut butter.

1 large onion, chopped

1 Tbsp olive oil

3 1/2 cups fat-free low-sodium or regular chicken broth

4 1/2 cups peeled and cubed (1/3-inch) sweet potatoes

1 Tbsp peeled and minced fresh gingerroot

1 tsp dried thyme leaves

1 tsp ground allspice

1/8 tsp hot red pepper flakes, or to taste

1 28-oz can crushed canned tomatoes in light puree

1/3 cup smooth peanut butter

Salt and black pepper to taste (optional)

PREP TIME: 20 MINUTES

SERVINGS: 9

SERVING SIZE: 1 CUP

Exchanges
1 1/2 Starch
1 Vegetable
1 Fat

Calories 184
   Calories from Fat 58
Total Fat . . . . .6 g
   Saturated Fat . . . . .1 g
Cholesterol . . . . .0 mg
Sodium . . . . .376 mg
Total Carbohydrate . . . .26 g
   Dietary Fiber . . . . .5 g
   Sugars . . . . .13 g
Protein . . . . .7 g

1 In a 4-quart saucepan or similar-size soup pot, combine the onion and oil. Cook over medium-high heat, stirring frequently, 3 or 4 minutes, until the onion is soft and beginning to brown.

2 Stir in the broth, sweet potatoes, gingerroot, thyme, allspice, and crushed red pepper. Bring to a boil over high heat. Reduce the heat; simmer, uncovered, stirring occasionally, until the sweet potatoes are just tender, 7 to 8 minutes.

3 Scoop up 3 1/2 cups vegetables, then 1 cup broth from pan and place in a food processor. Process until completely pureed and smooth. Return the pureed mixture to the saucepan.

4 Combine about two-thirds of the canned tomatoes and the peanut butter in the processor. Process until well blended. Return the pureed mixture, then the remaining tomatoes, to the saucepan.

5 Bring the mixture to a simmer. Cook 2 to 3 minutes longer, until the bisque is piping hot and the flavors are blended. Taste and add salt and pepper, if desired.

VEGETARIAN MINESTRONE

Try this meatless version of an Italian classic—updated for quick and easy preparation. If you like, you can make it with chicken broth instead of vegetable broth.

1 Tbsp extra-virgin olive oil

1 medium onion, finely chopped

1 tsp minced garlic

4 cups vegetable broth or bouillon, divided

1 15-oz can low-sodium or regular tomato sauce

1 19-oz can cannellini beans, rinsed and drained

1 large celery stalk, diced

6 baby carrots, sliced

1 1/2 cups diced zucchini

1/4 cup chopped fresh parsley leaves

1 1/2 tsp Italian seasoning

1/8 tsp ground celery seed

1/4 tsp black pepper

1/2 cup small elbow macaroni

Salt to taste (optional)

5 1/2 Tbsp grated Parmesan cheese

PREP TIME: 20 MINUTES

SERVINGS: 8

SERVING SIZE: 1 CUP

Exchanges
1 Starch
2 Vegetable
1/2 Fat

Calories 157
  Calories from Fat 34
Total Fat . . . . .4 g
  Saturated Fat . . . . .1 g
Cholesterol . . . . .5 mg
Sodium . . . . .645 mg
Total Carbohydrate . . . .24 g
  Dietary Fiber . . . . .5 g
  Sugars . . . . .7 g
Protein . . . . .8 g

1 In a Dutch oven or similar large pot, combine the oil, onion, garlic, and 3 table-spoons of the vegetable broth. Cook over medium heat, stirring frequently, for 5 or 6 minutes, until the onion is tender. If the liquid begins to evaporate, add a bit more broth.

2 Add the remaining broth, tomato sauce, beans, celery, carrots, and zucchini. Then add the parsley, Italian seasoning, celery seed, and pepper. Stir to mix well. Cover and bring to a boil. Lower the heat, and simmer about 15 minutes.

3 Bring the soup to a boil. Add the pasta. Lower the heat again, and simmer, uncovered, stirring occasionally, an additional 15 to 20 minutes or until the vegetables and pasta are tender.

4 As the pasta thickens the soup, stir to make sure it doesn't stick to the bottom of the pan. Add salt to taste, if desired. Sprinkle each portion with a scant 2 teaspoons of Parmesan cheese. This soup is best the day it's made, since the pasta tends to absorb the liquid. When reheating, add a bit more broth.

VEGETABLE AND SAUSAGE SOUP

Sausage gives this quick vegetable soup its appealing flavor.

3/4 *lb smoked, low-fat turkey sausage, sliced*

1 *cup chopped onion*

1 *tsp minced garlic*

1 *Tbsp olive oil*

3 1/2 *cups fat-free low-sodium or regular chicken broth, divided*

1 *15-oz can low-sodium or regular tomato sauce*

1 *16-oz can low-sodium or regular dark red kidney beans, drained*

2 *cups frozen broccoli, peppers, and corn*

1/4 *cup white rice*

1/4 *tsp dried thyme leaves*

1/4 *tsp black pepper*

1 In a Dutch oven or small soup pot, combine the sausage, onion, garlic, olive oil, and 2 tablespoons of broth. Cook over medium heat, stirring frequently, until the onions soften, about 5 or 6 minutes. Add all the remaining ingredients.

2 Bring the soup to a boil over high heat. Lower the heat, cover, and simmer, stirring occasionally, about 20 minutes or until the flavors are well blended and the soup has thickened slightly.

PREP TIME: 15 MINUTES

SERVINGS: 10

SERVING SIZE: 1 CUP

Exchanges
1 Starch
1 Medium-Fat Meat

Calories 148
  Calories from Fat 40
Total Fat . . . . .4 g
  Saturated Fat . . . . .1 g
Cholesterol . . . . .22 mg
Sodium . . . . .703 mg
Total Carbohydrate . . . .17 g
  Dietary Fiber . . . . .3 g
  Sugars . . . . .6 g
Protein . . . . .8 g

STEWS, CHILIS, CURRIES, AND HOT POTS

CHICKEN AND SHRIMP GUMBO

> This recipe calls for either okra or green beans. Okra is traditional in gumbo, but green beans may be substituted with good results.

3/4 lb boneless, skinless chicken breast, cut into 1-inch chunks

2 cups plus 3 Tbsp fat-free low-sodium or regular chicken broth, divided

1/2 tsp dried thyme leaves

1/4 tsp dried oregano leaves

1/4 tsp ground white pepper (or substitute black pepper), to taste

1 large clove garlic, peeled and minced

2 Tbsp olive oil, divided

1 cup 1/2-inch green onion pieces, including tender tops

1 large celery stalk, coarsely chopped

1 cup coarsely chopped red or green bell pepper

2 Tbsp all-purpose white flour

3/4 cup trimmed and sliced okra or cut green beans

1/2 lb fresh shrimp, peeled

2 cups hot cooked white or brown rice
Salt and black pepper to taste
(optional)

PREP TIME: 25 MINUTES

SERVINGS: 4

SERVING SIZE: 1 CUP GUMBO PLUS 1/2 CUP RICE

Exchanges
2 Starch
1 Vegetable
4 Very Lean Meat
1 Fat

Calories 365
  Calories from Fat 86
Total Fat . . . . .10 g
  Saturated Fat . . . . .2 g
Cholesterol . . . . .119 mg
Sodium . . . . .396 mg
Total Carbohydrate . . . .34 g
  Dietary Fiber . . . . .3 g
  Sugars . . . . .4 g
Protein . . . . .34 g

1 In a large bowl, combine the chicken, 3 tablespoons broth, thyme, oregano, white pepper, and garlic, stirring until chicken pieces are coated. Set aside.

2 In a 12-inch nonstick stir-fry pan or deep-sided skillet over medium-high heat, combine 1/2 tablespoon oil, the green onions, celery, and pepper, stirring. Cook until the green onions begin to brown, about 4 minutes. Stir in the chicken, thyme, oregano, and any remaining liquid. Raise heat to high and cook, stirring, until the chicken is lightly browned, about 4 minutes. Reserve the chicken and vegetables in a bowl.

3 Wipe out the skillet with a paper towel. Add the remaining 1 1/2 tablespoons oil to it. Stir in the flour. Cook, stirring constantly, over high heat until the mixture (called a roux) is well browned; adjust the heat if necessary to keep the roux from burning.

4 Slowly, but vigorously, stir in the remaining broth until the mixture is smooth. Stir in the okra or green beans, and reserved chicken and vegetables. Return to a simmer over medium-high heat. Simmer about 10 minutes or until the flavors are mingled.

5 Stir in the shrimp; continue cooking just until the shrimp are pink and curled, about 1 to 2 minutes longer. Add salt and pepper, if desired.

6 Spoon 1/2 cup rice into each soup plate. Spoon the gumbo over top.

QUICK CHICKEN CURRY

" This slightly spicy curry is one of our favorites. The raisin and peanut garnishes add pleasing chew and crunch. "

1 cup fat-free low-sodium or regular chicken broth, divided

2 1/2 Tbsp mild curry powder, divided

1 tsp dried thyme leaves

1 lb boneless, skinless chicken breast halves, cut into 1-inch cubes

2 Tbsp peanut oil or olive oil, divided

1 generous cup chopped onion

1 generous cup chopped celery

1 Tbsp all-purpose white flour

1 8-oz can tomato sauce

1/4 tsp salt (optional)

2 cups cooked long-grain brown or white rice

1/4 cup golden or brown raisins for garnish

1/4 cup coarsely chopped peanuts for garnish

PREP TIME: 20 MINUTES

SERVINGS: 4

SERVING SIZE: 1 CUP CURRY PLUS 1/2 CUP RICE AND 1 TBSP EACH RAISINS AND PEANUTS

Exchanges
2 Starch
1 Vegetable
4 Lean Meat
1/2 Fruit

Calories 446
   Calories from Fat . . .144
Total Fat . . . . .16 g
   Saturated Fat . . . . .3 g
Cholesterol . . . . .68 mg
Sodium . . . . .559 mg
Total Carbohydrate . . . .44 g
   Dietary Fiber . . . . .6 g
   Sugars . . . . .13 g
Protein . . . . .33 g

1 In a medium bowl make a seasoning paste by stirring together 2 tablespoons broth, 1 tablespoon curry powder, and the thyme. Stir in the chicken until coated; let stand for 5 to 10 minutes.

2 In a 12-inch nonstick skillet, heat 1 tablespoon oil over medium-high heat until hot but not smoking. Add the onion and celery; cook, stirring occasionally, until the onion is softened, about 4 minutes.

3 Stir the flour into the vegetable mixture until evenly incorporated. Add the remaining 1 tablespoon oil, the chicken pieces, and their seasoning mixture to the skillet. Adjust the heat so the chicken cooks rapidly but does not burn. Cook, turning frequently, until browned on all sides, about 5 to 8 minutes.

4 Stir the remaining chicken broth, tomato sauce, and 1 1/2 tablespoons more curry powder into the skillet. Lower the heat; simmer, stirring occasionally, 8 to 10 minutes longer, until the flavors blend and mixture cooks down a bit. Add salt, if desired. Spoon the curry over rice. Pass the curry garnishes at the table.

Chunky White Chili
with Chicken

For a bit of color and flavor, garnish the servings with chopped cilantro and some lime wedges on the side.

1 1/2 *cups fat-free low-sodium or regular chicken broth, divided*

1 1/4 *tsp mild to medium-hot chili powder*

1 1/4 *tsp dried oregano leaves*

1 *tsp dried thyme leaves*

2 *large whole bay leaves*

1/4 *tsp hot pepper sauce, or to taste*

4 *4-oz boneless, skinless chicken breast halves*

1 1/2 *Tbsp olive oil*

1 *large onion, chopped*

2 *large stalks celery, chopped*

2 *14- to 15-oz cans great northern white beans, rinsed and drained*

1 to 3 *Tbsp fresh lime juice, to taste*

Salt to taste (optional)

Cilantro leaves, chopped, and lime wedges for garnish (optional)

PREP TIME: 20 MINUTES

SERVINGS: 6

SERVING SIZE: 1 CUP

Exchanges
1 Starch
1 Vegetable
4 Very Lean Meat
1/2 Fat

Calories 258
    Calories from Fat 45
Total Fat . . . . .5 g
    Saturated Fat . . . . .1 g
Cholesterol . . . . .53 mg
Sodium . . . . .361 mg
Total Carbohydrate . . . .23 g
    Dietary Fiber . . . . .7 g
    Sugars . . . . .5 g
Protein . . . . .30 g

1 In a medium bowl, thoroughly stir together 3/4 cup broth, the chili powder, oregano, thyme, bay leaves, and hot pepper sauce. Cut the chicken breast halves in thirds lengthwise. Add to the bowl; let stand 5 minutes.

2 Meanwhile, in a 12-inch or larger deep-sided skillet or stir-fry pan over medium-high heat, combine the oil, onion, and celery, and cook until the onion is soft, stirring occasionally, about 5 minutes.

3 Stir in the chicken pieces and broth mixture. Simmer, stirring, about 6 or 7 minutes longer, until the chicken pieces are barely cooked through. Remove the chicken pieces and let stand until cool enough to handle.

4 Stir the remaining broth and the beans into the skillet. Simmer, uncovered, 5 to 8 minutes to allow flavors to blend.

5 Meanwhile, cut the chicken into bite-sized chunks, or pull it into chunks using forks. Return it to the skillet; simmer until piping hot, about 3 minutes longer. Remove the bay leaves and discard. Add the lime juice and salt to taste. Garnish the servings with cilantro and lime wedges, if desired.

THREE-BEAN CHILI

" Although chili is traditionally made with kidney beans, you can mix and match varieties, as this tasty version proves. "

1 lb lean ground beef

2 cups finely chopped onion

1 tsp minced garlic

1 19-oz can white kidney beans or cannellini beans, rinsed and well drained

1 16-oz can light-skinned low-sodium red kidney beans, rinsed and drained

1 16-oz can black beans, rinsed and drained

1 16-oz jar mild salsa

1 15-oz can low-sodium tomato sauce or regular tomato sauce

1 14 1/2-oz can low-sodium diced tomatoes

1 Tbsp plus 1 tsp chili powder

2 tsp granulated sugar

1 1/2 tsp ground cumin

1/8 tsp black pepper

Salt to taste (optional)

PREP TIME: 20 MINUTES

SERVINGS: 10

SERVING SIZE: 1 CUP

Exchanges
1 1/2 Starch
2 Vegetable
1/2 Fat
1 Medium-Fat Meat

Calories 264
   Calories from Fat 61
Total Fat . . . . .7 g
   Saturated Fat . . . . .2 g
Cholesterol . . . . .28 mg
Sodium . . . . .259 mg
Total Carbohydrate . . . .34 g
   Dietary Fiber . . . . . . .10 g
   Sugars . . . . .9 g
Protein . . . . .18 g

1 In a Dutch oven or similar large heavy pot, combine the ground beef, onion, and garlic. Cook over medium heat, stirring frequently, until the beef has changed color. Drain fat.

2 Add the beans, salsa, tomato sauce, diced tomatoes, chili powder, sugar, cumin, black pepper, and salt, if desired.

3 Bring to a boil. Reduce the heat, cover, and simmer 45 minutes to 1 hour, stirring occasionally, until flavors are well blended.

ROADHOUSE CHILI

Here's a tasty chili variation with chunky texture. Incidentally, since the recipe relies on commercial salsa, which is fairly high in salt, this is one dish where it's really best to use low-sodium beans.

1 lb lean, thin-cut round steak, trimmed of fat

1/2 cup finely chopped onion

1 tsp minced garlic

2 Tbsp olive oil

3 cans light-skinned low-sodium or regular kidney beans, drained

1 1/2 cups mild or medium salsa

2 15-oz cans low-sodium or regular tomato sauce

1 Tbsp chili powder, or to taste

1 tsp ground cumin

1 tsp granulated sugar

1/8 tsp black pepper

Salt to taste (optional)

PREP TIME: 20 MINUTES

SERVINGS: 9

SERVING SIZE: 1 CUP

Exchanges
1 1/2 Starch
2 Lean Meat
1 Vegetable

Calories 247
    Calories from Fat 51
Total Fat . . . . .6 g
    Saturated Fat . . . . .1 g
Cholesterol . . . . .26 mg
Sodium . . . . .161 mg
Total Carbohydrate . . . .30 g
    Dietary Fiber . . . . .9 g
    Sugars . . . . .7 g
Protein . . . . .18 g

1 Cut the round steak into thin slices. Then cut across the slices to make small pieces. In a Dutch oven or similar large heavy pot, combine the round steak, onion, garlic, and oil. Cook over medium heat, stirring frequently, until the beef has changed color.

2 Add the kidney beans, salsa, tomato sauce, chili powder, cumin, sugar, black pepper, and salt, if desired.

3 Bring to a boil. Reduce heat, cover, and simmer 45 minutes to 1 hour, stirring occasionally, until the flavors are well blended. Serve in bowls.

"STUFFED PEPPERS" STEW

This homey dish has the taste of stuffed green peppers, but no peppers get stuffed! Instead, all the ingredients are cooked up in an easy, home-style stew. The yield is large, but the stew keeps well for several days.

1 lb extra-lean ground beef

1 large onion, very coarsely chopped

1 tsp ground allspice

4 medium green or red bell peppers (or a combination), cored, seeded, and cut into 1-inch chunks

1 28-oz can stewed tomatoes, including juice

1 15-oz can low-sodium tomato sauce

3 beef bouillon cubes or 3 tsp beef bouillon granules, dissolved in 1/2 cup hot water

2/3 cup uncooked long-grain white rice

1/4 tsp black pepper, to taste

1/4 tsp salt (optional)

1 to 2 tsp sugar, to taste (optional)

PREP TIME: 25 MINUTES

SERVINGS: 11

SERVING SIZE: 1 CUP

Exchanges
1/2 Starch
3 Vegetable
1 Lean Meat

Calories 173
   Calories from Fat 48
Total Fat . . . . .5 g
   Saturated Fat . . . . .2 g
Cholesterol . . . . .26 mg
Sodium . . . . .464 mg
Total Carbohydrate . . . .22 g
   Dietary Fiber . . . . .3 g
   Sugars . . . . .7 g
Protein . . . . .10 g

1 In a 4-quart or larger saucepan or pot over medium-high heat, combine the beef, onion, and allspice. Stirring the beef to break it up as much as possible, cook for 5 minutes until lightly browned.

2 Stir in the peppers, tomatoes, tomato sauce, bouillon-water mixture, rice, and black pepper. Bring to a boil.

3 Adjust the heat so the stew simmers gently, and cook, covered and stirring occasionally, 25 to 30 minutes or until the rice is just cooked through.

4 Taste and add salt and more pepper, if desired. If the stew has a noticeable acidity due to the tomatoes, also stir in a little sugar, to taste.

MINCED BEEF CURRY WITH SAFFRON

Saffron adds a distinctive flavor and color to this very aromatic curry, so don't omit it. Add a leafy green salad to round out the meal.

2/3 lb extra-lean ground beef

3 medium celery ribs, chopped

1 large onion or medium red onion, chopped

1 cup diced red or green bell pepper, or chopped broccoli florets

1 Tbsp corn oil or canola oil

1 Tbsp mild or medium curry powder

1 1/2 tsp mild or medium chili powder

2 tsp finely chopped fresh gingerroot

1/8 tsp saffron threads, thoroughly crumbled

3 Tbsp lite soy sauce

1/2 cup low-sodium or regular tomato sauce combined with 1/2 cup hot water

1/4 cup golden raisins

2 cups hot cooked brown or white rice

Chopped cilantro leaves for garnish (optional)

PREP TIME: 20 MINUTES

SERVINGS: 4

SERVING SIZE: 1 CUP CURRY, PLUS 1/2 CUP RICE

Exchanges
2 1/2 Starch
1 Vegetable
2 Lean Meat

Calories 310
    Calories from Fat 54
Total Fat . . . . .6 g
    Saturated Fat . . . . .1 g
Cholesterol . . . . .40 mg
Sodium . . . . .561 mg
Total Carbohydrate . . . .44 g
    Dietary Fiber . . . . .6 g
    Sugars . . . . .13 g
Protein . . . . .20 g

1 Combine the beef, celery, onion, bell pepper, and oil in a 12-inch nonstick stir-fry pan or deep-sided nonstick skillet over high heat; stirring and breaking up the beef with a spoon. Stir in the curry powder, chili powder, ginger, and saffron threads. Cook, stirring, until the beef is lightly browned and the vegetables are limp, about 5 minutes longer.

2 Stir in the soy sauce, tomato sauce mixture, and raisins. Lower the heat so the curry simmers gently and cook, stirring occasionally, about 10 minutes longer or until the flavors are well blended. If necessary, add a few tablespoons water to prevent the sauce from becoming too thick.

3 Spoon the curry over the rice. Garnish with cilantro, if desired.

BEEF PAPRIKASH

Here's a rich and flavorful stew that's wonderful on a cold winter night. We brown the beef cubes the easy way—under the broiler, along with the onion and garlic. Be sure to cut the beef into small pieces so they cook quickly.

1 1/2 lb *lean stew beef, trimmed of fat and cut into small bite-sized pieces*

Salt and pepper to taste

1 *cup chopped onion*

1 *tsp minced garlic*

1 8-oz *can low-sodium or regular tomato sauce*

1 1/2 *cups fat-free low-sodium or regular chicken broth, divided*

15 or 20 *baby carrots*

2 *large celery stalks, sliced*

1 *cup thinly sliced cabbage*

1 Tbsp *paprika*

1 *tsp dried thyme leaves*

1 *cup nonfat sour cream*

6 oz *egg noodles, cooked according to package directions (about 1 2/3 cups)*

PREP TIME: 15 MINUTES

SERVINGS: 6

SERVING SIZE: 1 CUP, PLUS 1 OZ NOODLES

Exchanges
2 Starch
3 Lean Meat
1 Vegetable

Calories 351
   Calories from Fat 71
Total Fat . . . . .8 g
   Saturated Fat . . . . .3 g
Cholesterol . . . . .105 mg
Sodium . . . . .257 mg
Total Carbohydrate . . . .36 g
   Dietary Fiber . . . . .3 g
   Sugars . . . . .10 g
Protein . . . . .32 g

1 Preheat the broiler. Adjust the rack about 4 inches from the heating element. Sprinkle the meat with salt and pepper. Tuck the onion and garlic among the meat pieces. Broil about 10 to 12 minutes, stirring several times, until the meat is browned on all sides.

2 Meanwhile, in a Dutch oven or similar large pot, combine the tomato sauce with all but a few tablespoons of the broth. Stir to mix well. Add the carrots, celery, and cabbage. Stir in the paprika and thyme.

3 Transfer the meat mixture to the Dutch oven. Pour the remaining broth into the pan used for browning the meat, and stir up any bits of meat and vegetables that have stuck to the pan. Transfer to the Dutch oven.

4 Bring to a boil. Reduce the heat and simmer 1 to 1 1/2 hours, with the lid ajar, or until the vegetables and meat are tender. Stir occasionally and check to make sure the sauce isn't sticking to the bottom of the pot or boiling away. If the sauce becomes too thick, add a bit of water.

5 Remove the pot from the heat. Stir in sour cream. Add salt and pepper to taste, if desired. Serve over cooked noodles.

STICK-TO-THE-RIBS BEEF STEW

A good stew is worth a king's ransom. It's also worth using fresh ingredients. This flavorful example is perfect for dinner on a cold winter evening. To speed preparation and eliminate the oil ordinarily used in browning, we coat the beef cubes with flour and brown them under the broiler, along with the onion and garlic. Be sure to cut the beef into small pieces so the cubes cook quickly.

1 1/2 Tbsp white flour

1 lb lean stew beef, trimmed of all fat and cut into small bite-sized pieces

1 cup finely chopped onion

1 tsp minced garlic

2 1/2 cups fat-free low-sodium or regular chicken broth, divided

1 15-oz can low-sodium or regular tomato sauce

1 cup baby carrots

3 large celery stalks, sliced

2 cups 2-inch fresh green bean pieces

3/4 lb medium boiling potatoes, peeled and quartered (about 4 cups)

1 tsp dried thyme leaves

1 tsp dried basil leaves

2 large bay leaves

1/4 tsp salt, or to taste (optional)

1/4 tsp black pepper

PREP TIME: 25 MINUTES

SERVINGS: 4

SERVING SIZE: 2 1/4 CUPS

Exchanges
1 Starch
4 Vegetable
2 Lean Meat

Calories 285
   Calories from Fat 37
Total Fat . . . . .4 g
   Saturated Fat . . . . .1 g
Cholesterol . . . . .52 mg
Sodium . . . . .449 mg
Total Carbohydrate . . . .35 g
   Dietary Fiber . . . . .7 g
   Sugars . . . . .14 g
Protein . . . . .27 g

1 Preheat the broiler. Adjust the rack about 2 inches from the heating element. Coat a shallow baking pan with nonstick spray. Sprinkle the flour over the meat. Stir to coat. Stir in onion and garlic. Spread out the mixture so that the meat pieces are separated from one another. Broil about 12 to 15 minutes, stirring once or twice, until the meat is browned on all sides.

2 Transfer the meat mixture to a Dutch oven or similar large, heavy pot. Pour some of the broth into the pan and stir up any bits of meat, flour, and vegetables that have stuck to the pan. Transfer to the Dutch oven.

3 Add the remaining broth and tomato sauce. Stir to mix well. Add the carrots, celery, green beans, and potatoes. Stir in the thyme, basil, bay leaves, salt, if desired, and pepper.

4 Bring to a boil. Cover, reduce the heat, and simmer about 1 hour, or until the vegetables and meat are tender. Stir occasionally and check to make sure the gravy isn't sticking to the bottom of the pot. Remove bay leaves.

GROUND BEEF AND CABBAGE STEW

This very satisfying dish reminds us of stuffed cabbage—but involves far less work.

3/4 lb extra lean ground beef

2 medium onions, chopped

4 cups fat-free reduced-sodium or
  regular chicken broth

1 15-oz can salt-free or regular tomato
  sauce

3 cups shredded cabbage, excluding
  coarse ribs

1/2 cup (uncooked) white basmati rice

1/2 large green bell pepper, seeded and
  chopped

2 tsp granulated sugar

1 1/2 tsp dried thyme leaves

1 tsp apple cider vinegar

1 large bay leaf

1/4 tsp ground allspice

1/4 tsp black pepper

Salt to taste (optional)

PREP TIME: 20 MINUTES

SERVINGS: 6

SERVING SIZE: 1 1/2 CUPS

Exchanges
1 Vegetable
1 Starch
1 Very Lean Meat

Calories 158
    Calories from Fat 18
Total Fat . . . . .2 g
    Saturated Fat . . . . .1 g
Cholesterol . . . . .30 mg
Sodium . . . . .348 mg
Total Carbohydrate . . . .21 g
    Dietary Fiber . . . . .3 g
    Sugars . . . . .8 g
Protein . . . . .14 g

1 In a large Dutch oven or similar large, heavy pot, combine the ground beef and onion. Cook over medium heat, stirring frequently, until the beef loses its pink color.

2 Add the broth, tomato sauce, cabbage, rice, green pepper, sugar, thyme, vinegar, bay leaf, allspice, and black pepper. Stir to mix well.

3 Cover and bring to a boil. Reduce the heat and simmer, stirring occasionally, 20 to 30 minutes or until the rice is just tender. Add salt, if desired.

SWEDISH MEATBALLS

" We brown these tasty meatballs in the oven to speed the preparation. You can make the sauce while they're cooking. "

MEATBALLS

    1 *lb ground beef round*

  1/4 *tsp salt, or to taste (optional)*

    1 *Tbsp instant minced onions*

    1 *tsp minced garlic*

    1 *egg white*

  1/4 *cup quick-cooking or old-fashioned rolled oats*

  1/2 *tsp ground allspice*

  1/2 *tsp ground ginger*

SAUCE

    1 *medium onion, finely chopped*

  1/2 *lb fresh mushrooms, washed, trimmed, and sliced*

 2 1/2 *Tbsp olive oil*

 1 1/4 *cups defatted beef broth*

 1 1/4 *tsp dried thyme leaves*

 1 1/2 *tsp Dijon-style mustard*

  1/4 *tsp black pepper*

  1/4 *tsp salt, or to taste (optional)*

  1/2 *cup quick-cooking rice*

  3/4 *cup nonfat sour cream*

     Parsley sprigs for garnish (optional)

PREP TIME: 25 MINUTES

SERVINGS: 4

SERVING SIZE: 1 CUP

Exchanges
1 1/2 Starch
1 Vegetable
1/2 Fat
3 Lean Meat

Calories 342
   Calories from Fat . . .104
Total Fat . . . . .12 g
   Saturated Fat . . . . .3 g
Cholesterol . . . . .61 mg
Sodium . . . . .631 mg
Total Carbohydrate . . . .28 g
   Dietary Fiber . . . . .2 g
   Sugars . . . . .7 g
Protein . . . . .30 g

1 Preheat the oven to 375 degrees. In a large bowl, combine all the meatball ingredients and mix well. Roll into 1-inch balls. Place the balls in a shallow baking pan or cookie sheets with sides. Bake in preheated oven for 15 minutes or until browned on all sides.

2 Meanwhile, in a large nonstick skillet, brown the onion and mushrooms in the oil over medium-high heat, stirring frequently, about 6 or 7 minutes or until the onion is tender.

3 Stir in the broth. Add the thyme, mustard, pepper, and salt, if desired, and stir to mix well. Add the meatballs. Cover and simmer 15 minutes, stirring occasionally, or until the flavors are well blended.

4 Add the rice, and cook an additional 5 minutes.

5 Carefully stir the sour cream into the broth. Heat 2 or 3 minutes longer. Garnish with parsley sprigs, if desired.

SMOKED PORK AND VEGETABLE HOT POT

Easy, savory, and filling, this makes a fine cool-weather meal.

3 cups fat-free low-sodium or regular
  chicken broth

1 medium onion, cut into eighths

1 large celery stalk, cut crosswise into
  1/2-inch pieces

1 large carrot, cut crosswise into 1/4-inch
  slices

2 cups very coarsely cubed red bliss or
  other thin-skinned boiling potatoes

1/2 tsp dried thyme leaves

1 large bay leaf

1 lb package boneless smoked pork chops,
  trimmed and cut into 3/4-inch cubes

2 1/2 cups frozen (thawed) cut green beans

2 cups fresh or frozen (thawed)
  cauliflower florets

Salt and black pepper to taste (optional)

PREP TIME: 20 MINUTES

SERVINGS: 7

SERVING SIZE: 1 CUP

Exchanges
1/2 Starch
2 Vegetable
1/2 Fat
1 Lean Meat

Calories 171
  Calories from Fat 43
Total Fat . . . . .5 g
  Saturated Fat . . . . . . .1 g
Cholesterol . . . . .34 mg
Sodium . . . . .929 mg
Total Carbohydrate . . . .19 g
  Dietary Fiber . . . . .4 g
  Sugars . . . . .5 g
Protein . . . . .15 g

1 In a very large saucepan or similar size pot, combine the broth, onion, celery, carrot, potatoes, thyme, and bay leaf. Bring to a simmer over medium-high heat; cook, uncovered, for 8 minutes.

2 Add the smoked pork cubes and green beans. Cover and cook 5 minutes longer.

3 Arrange the cauliflower over top; cover and cook until the florets are just tender when tested with a fork. Add salt and pepper to taste, if desired.

TUNA, PASTA, AND BROCCOLI CASSEROLE

" With some innovative techniques, we can give you tuna casserole in no time flat. "

2 cups uncooked penne or other similar
   pasta shape

3 cups small broccoli florets

1 medium onion, chopped

2 Tbsp fat-free low-sodium or regular
   chicken broth

1 Tbsp olive oil

1 1/2 Tbsp white flour

1 1/2 cups reduced-fat milk

1/2 tsp dried thyme leaves

1/2 tsp dried basil leaves

1/8 tsp white pepper

1/4 tsp salt, or to taste (optional)

2 6 1/2-oz cans water-packed tuna,
   drained and flaked

1 cup shredded reduced-fat cheddar
   cheese

PREP TIME: 15 MINUTES

SERVINGS: 8

SERVING SIZE: 1 CUP

Exchanges
1 Starch
1 Vegetable
2 Lean Meat

Calories 219
   Calories from Fat 53
Total Fat . . . . .6 g
   Saturated Fat . . . . .3 g
Cholesterol . . . . .23 mg
Sodium . . . . .300 mg
Total Carbohydrate . . . .22 g
   Dietary Fiber . . . . .2 g
   Sugars . . . . .4 g
Protein . . . . .20 g

1 In a large saucepan, bring 3 quarts of water to a boil. Add penne and cook 5 or 6 minutes. Add broccoli and boil an additional 3 to 4 minutes, or until pasta is tender. Drain in a colander. Then transfer to a 2 1/2-quart microwave-safe casserole dish.

2 In the saucepan, combine the onion, chicken broth, and oil. Cook over medium heat, stirring frequently, for 6 to 7 minutes or until the onion is tender. If the liquid begins to evaporate, add more broth.

3 Stir in the flour, and stir to make a smooth paste. Gradually add the milk, stirring constantly to make sure the mixture remains smooth. Cook until the milk has thickened. Add the thyme, basil, pepper, and salt, if desired. Stir to mix. Reduce the heat to low. Cook 1 minute longer, stirring. Stir in the tuna, and continue to cook an additional 1 or 2 minutes. Stir in the cheese.

4 Stir the sauce into the pasta-broccoli mixture. Cover with the casserole lid, and microwave 4 or 5 minutes until the casserole is hot.

GINGER-SHRIMP CURRY

In contrast to typical Indian curries, this one contains soy sauce and sesame oil and is East Asian in flavor. It is fragrant and slightly spicy with ginger.

1 *12-oz package peeled and cooked frozen (thawed) medium shrimp*

2 *Tbsp lite soy sauce*

2 *Tbsp tomato ketchup or chili sauce*

1 1/2 *Tbsp oriental sesame oil, divided*

1 1/2 *tsp mild to medium-hot curry powder*

1 1/2 *tsp minced fresh gingerroot*

1 1/4 *cups coarsely chopped red or green bell pepper*

1 1/4 *cups peeled and coarsely chopped Golden Delicious or similar sweet, flavorful apple*

1 *large onion, chopped*

1 1/2 *Tbsp all-purpose white flour*

2/3 *cup fat-free low-sodium or regular chicken broth*

Salt to taste

2 *cups hot cooked long-grain white rice*

1/4 *cup chopped peanuts for garnish (optional)*

PREP TIME: 15 MINUTES

SERVINGS: 4

SERVING SIZE: 1 CUP CURRY, PLUS 1/2 CUP RICE

Exchanges
2 Starch
2 Vegetable
1 Fat
2 Very Lean Meat

Calories 313
   Calories from Fat 60
Total Fat . . . . .7 g
   Saturated Fat . . . . .1 g
Cholesterol . . . . .165 mg
Sodium . . . . .669 mg
Total Carbohydrate . . . .41 g
   Dietary Fiber . . . . .3 g
   Sugars . . . . .11 g
Protein . . . . .22 g

1 In a medium bowl, stir together the shrimp, soy sauce, ketchup, 1/2 tablespoon oil, curry powder, and gingerroot. Let stand for 10 minutes.

2 In a 12-inch or larger nonstick skillet, heat the remaining 1 tablespoon oil to hot but not smoking over high heat. Add the peppers, apple, and onion. Adjust the heat so mixture cooks rapidly but does not burn, and cook, stirring, until the onions are lightly browned, 3 to 5 minutes.

3 Stir in the flour until evenly incorporated; cook 1 minute, stirring.

4 Stir in the shrimp and their seasoning mixture. Cook, stirring frequently, until the shrimp are just heated through. Stir in the chicken broth; heat just to piping hot. Add salt to taste.

5 Serve over rice, garnished with peanuts, if desired.

SERVED OVER PASTA

CHICKEN CACCIATORE

"Here's a quick and easy version of an old Italian favorite."

2 Tbsp olive oil, divided

1 large onion, chopped

8 oz white mushrooms, cleaned and sliced

1 tsp minced garlic

1 cup fat-free low-sodium or regular chicken broth, divided

3/4 lb skinless, boneless chicken breast, cut into bite-sized pieces

1 1/2 Tbsp all-purpose white flour

1/4 tsp salt (optional)

1/4 tsp black pepper

1 15-oz can Italian-style chunky tomato sauce

1 green bell pepper, seeded and cut into strips

1 tsp Italian seasoning

6 oz thin spaghetti, cooked according to package directions

3 Tbsp grated Parmesan cheese

PREP TIME: 20 MINUTES

SERVINGS: 6

SERVING SIZE: 1 CUP, PLUS 1 OZ PASTA

Exchanges
2 1/2 Starch
1 Vegetable
3 Very Lean Meat

Calories 349
 Calories from Fat 45
Total Fat . . . . .5 g
 Saturated Fat . . . . .1 g
Cholesterol . . . . .49 mg
Sodium . . . . .829 mg
Total Carbohydrate . . . .46 g
 Dietary Fiber . . . . .5 g
 Sugars . . . . .3 g
Protein . . . . .30 g

1 In a Dutch oven or similar large, heavy pot, combine 1 tablespoon of the oil, the onion, mushrooms, garlic, and 3 tablespoons of the broth. Cook over medium heat, stirring frequently, 5 or 6 minutes, or until the onion is tender. With a slotted spoon, remove the vegetables to a medium bowl and reserve.

2 Sprinkle the chicken with flour, salt, if desired, and pepper. Add the remaining oil to the pot. In the pot, cook chicken pieces over medium heat, turning frequently, until they begin to brown.

3 Return the vegetables to the pot. Add the tomato sauce, remaining chicken broth, green pepper, and Italian seasoning.

4 Cover and simmer 15 minutes, stirring occasionally. Taste the sauce and add additional salt and pepper if desired. Serve individual portions of chicken and sauce over pasta. Sprinkle 2 teaspoons of Parmesan cheese over each.

TURKEY SKILLET WITH SUN-DRIED TOMATOES AND OLIVES

"The sun-dried tomatoes give this dish a distinctive, rich tomato flavor and color. For the right flavor with less fat, be sure to use the dry-packed tomatoes and not bottled ones that are packed in oil."

1/4 cup dry-packed, sun-dried tomatoes

4 4-oz turkey breast cutlets

1 tsp balsamic vinegar

1 1/2 Tbsp olive oil, divided

1 tsp dried marjoram leaves

1/4 tsp garlic salt

2 cups frozen (thawed) mixed red, green, and yellow bell peppers and onion medley

3 Tbsp coarsely chopped, pitted black Nicoise or Kalamata olives

1 8-oz can low-sodium tomato sauce

Salt and black pepper to taste (optional)

2 cups hot cooked ziti, penne, or other medium-sized tube-shaped pasta

---

PREP TIME: 20 MINUTES

SERVINGS: 4

SERVING SIZE: 4-OZ CUTLET, 1/2 CUP VEGETABLES AND SAUCE, AND 1/2 CUP PASTA

Exchanges
1 1/2 Starch
2 Vegetable
3 Very Lean Meat
1 Fat

Calories 312
  Calories from Fat 59
Total Fat . . . . .7 g
  Saturated Fat . . . . .1 g
Cholesterol . . . . .73 mg
Sodium . . . . .202 mg
Total Carbohydrate . . . .30 g
  Dietary Fiber . . . . .3 g
  Sugars . . . . .8 g
Protein . . . . .32 g

1 In a small bowl or cup combine the sun-dried tomatoes with 1/3 cup boiling water. Let stand while the remaining ingredients are readied.

2 In a medium, non-reactive bowl, thoroughly stir together the turkey cutlets, vinegar, 1/2 tablespoon oil, marjoram, and garlic salt. Let stand for 5 minutes.

3 In a 12-inch nonstick skillet, heat the remaining 1 tablespoon oil over high heat until hot but not smoking. Add the turkey cutlets (and any leftover seasonings in bowl). Reduce heat slightly; continue cooking until the cutlets are colored all over, about 3 minutes.

4 Add the pepper-onion medley, olives, and tomato sauce to the cutlets. Chop the sun-dried tomatoes; reserve their liquid. Add the sun-dried tomatoes and their liquid to the skillet. Simmer, stirring occasionally, until the flavors are well blended, about 3 minutes longer.

5 Add salt and pepper to taste, if desired. Lay the cutlets over pasta. Spoon the vegetables and sauce over top.

ROUND STEAK PIZZAIOLA

Here's a traditional Italian-style dinner. Since seasoned tomato sauce varies greatly in sugar and salt content, be sure to check labels carefully. And be sure to use thin-sliced round steak, because it cooks more quickly than thicker cuts.

3/4 lb thin-cut round steak, trimmed
    of all fat and cut into small strips

1/4 tsp salt (optional)

1/8 tsp black pepper

1 cup chopped onion

1 large green bell pepper, seeded and
    chopped

2 cups sliced mushrooms

1/3 cup fat-free reduced-sodium or regular
    chicken broth, divided

1 Tbsp olive oil

1 1/2 cups reduced-fat Italian-seasoned
    spaghetti or marinara sauce

1 1/2 cups (6 oz) uncooked penne or similar
    pasta shape

3 Tbsp grated Parmesan cheese, divided

PREP TIME: 20 MINUTES

SERVINGS: 4

SERVING SIZE: 1 CUP MEAT
    AND VEGETABLES,
    PLUS PASTA

Exchanges
3 Starch
1 Vegetable
3 Lean Meat

Calories 414
    Calories from Fat 90
Total Fat . . . . .10 g
    Saturated Fat . . . . .2 g
Cholesterol . . . . .51 mg
Sodium . . . . .513 mg
Total Carbohydrate . . . .50 g
    Dietary Fiber . . . . .4 g
    Sugars . . . . .7 g
Protein . . . . .31 g

1 Sprinkle the round steak with salt, if desired, and pepper. In a 12-inch nonstick skillet coated with nonstick spray, cook the round steak over medium heat until browned on all sides, stirring frequently, about 4 to 5 minutes. Remove with a slotted spoon and reserve.

2 In the skillet, combine the onion, green pepper, mushrooms, 2 tablespoons of the broth, and oil. Cook over medium heat, stirring frequently, until the onion is tender, about 5 to 6 minutes.

3 Return the meat to the pan. Add the spaghetti sauce and remaining broth. Stir to mix well. Bring to a boil. Reduce heat, cover, and simmer 20 to 25 minutes until meat is tender.

4 Meanwhile, cook the pasta according to package directions without added fat or salt. Add the pasta to sauce, and stir to mix well. Serve from the skillet. Sprinkle each serving with grated Parmesan cheese.

EASY ITALIAN-STYLE PORK CHOP AND ZUCCHINI DINNER

" We especially like the chops seasoned with rosemary, although oregano can be substituted if that's what you have on hand. "

1 Tbsp olive oil

4 4-oz well-trimmed boneless loin pork chops

1/2 tsp crumbled dried rosemary, or dried oregano leaves

1/8 to 1/4 tsp salt for seasoning chops

1 small onion, chopped

1 large clove garlic, peeled and minced

2 1/2 cups 1/4 inch–thick slices zucchini

2 cups commercial tomato pasta sauce

Black pepper to taste (optional)

4 oz whole-wheat or regular spaghetti, cooked according to package directions

PREP TIME: 20 MINUTES

SERVINGS: 4

SERVING SIZE: 1 PORK CHOP, 1 CUP ZUCCHINI AND SAUCE, AND 1 OZ SPAGHETTI

Exchanges
3 Carbohydrate
2 Lean Meat
1/2 Fat

Calories 369
   Calories from Fat . . .111
Total Fat . . . . .12 g
   Saturated Fat . . . . .3 g
Cholesterol . . . . .47 mg
Sodium . . . . .596 mg
Total Carbohydrate . . . .43 g
   Dietary Fiber . . . . .8 g
   Sugars . . . . .6 g
Protein . . . . .24 g

1 Heat the oil in a 12-inch nonstick skillet over medium-high heat. Add the pork chops and sprinkle both sides with the rosemary (or oregano) and salt. Cook the chops, turning occasionally, until well browned on both sides, about 6 or 7 minutes.

2 Add the onion, garlic, and zucchini slices, and continue cooking until the onions are soft, about 5 or 6 minutes longer.

3 Add the pasta sauce, stirring until it is well combined with the chops and vegetables. Add black pepper, if desired. Adjust the heat so the sauce simmers gently and cook 6 to 8 minutes longer, or until the zucchini slices are crisp-tender and the chops are just cooked through, tested in the thickest part with the point of a paring knife.

4 Serve the chops and zucchini-sauce mixture over the pasta.

Fresh Tomato Sauce with Clams over Pasta

For best results, use fragrant, fully ripe, peak-of-season summer tomatoes in this recipe.

6 or 7 large, flavorful sun-ripened tomatoes (enough to yield 4 cups peeled, cored, and chopped)

1 1/2 Tbsp olive oil

1/4 cup chopped onion

1/4 cup chopped red bell pepper

1 large clove garlic, peeled and minced

1 10 1/2-oz can whole baby clams (or minced clams), including juice

1/4 tsp black pepper, or to taste

1/4 tsp salt, or to taste

8 oz hot whole-wheat or regular spaghetti, cooked according to package directions

PREP TIME: 20 MINUTES

SERVINGS: 4

SERVING SIZE: 3/4 CUP SAUCE, PLUS 2 OZ PASTA

Exchanges
1 Starch
3 Vegetable
1 Very Lean Meat
1 Fat

Calories 216
   Calories from Fat 57
Total Fat . . . . .6 g
   Saturated Fat . . . . .1 g
Cholesterol . . . . .23 mg
Sodium . . . . .288 mg
Total Carbohydrate . . . .30 g
   Dietary Fiber . . . . .3 g
   Sugars . . . . .9 g
Protein . . . . .13 g

1 Bring a large saucepan half full of water to a boil. Core the tomatoes. Slip the tomatoes into the water and let them heat for 1 minute or until their skins loosen. Immediately remove them to a large bowl using tongs or a slotted spoon. Let stand until cool enough to handle. Then peel off and discard the skins. Coarsely chop the tomatoes; you need 4 cups of pulp.

2 Combine the oil, onion, and bell pepper in a 12-inch or larger nonstick skillet over medium-high heat. Cook, stirring, until the onions are soft and just beginning to brown, about 2 minutes. Add the garlic and cook, stirring, 1 minute longer.

3 Stir the tomatoes and the juice from the clams into the skillet. Adjust the heat so the mixture boils briskly. Cook, uncovered, stirring frequently, until it begins to thicken, about 10 to 12 minutes. Stirring frequently to prevent sticking, continue cooking until the mixture cooks down to a thick, chunky puree, about 4 minutes longer.

4 Stir the clams and black pepper into the tomato mixture. Taste and add salt, if desired. Heat till piping hot; spoon the sauce over the pasta.

CODFISH FLORENTINE STYLE

Be sure to use fish filets that are at least 1/2-inch thick for this tasty recipe.

4 oz uncooked penne or other similar pasta shape (about 1 1/4 cups)

1/4 tsp salt (optional)

1/8 tsp black pepper

1 lb fresh or frozen (thawed) skinless codfish filets

1 Tbsp olive oil

1 15-oz can Italian-style chunky tomato sauce

1 cup chopped frozen spinach, thawed and well drained

1 tsp minced garlic

2 Tbsp grated Parmesan cheese

PREP TIME: 10 MINUTES

SERVINGS: 4

SERVING SIZE: 4 OZ FISH, PLUS 1 OZ PASTA AND SAUCE

Exchanges
1 1/2 Starch
3 Vegetable
3 Very Lean Meat
1/2 Fat

Calories 325
   Calories from Fat 56
Total Fat . . . . .6 g
   Saturated Fat . . . . .1 g
Cholesterol . . . . .54 mg
Sodium . . . . .913 mg
Total Carbohydrate . . . .37 g
   Dietary Fiber . . . . .4 g
   Sugars . . . . .13 g
Protein . . . . .31 g

1 Cook pasta according to package directions. Rinse and drain in a colander. Reserve.

2 Meanwhile, sprinkle salt, if desired, and black pepper evenly over fish.

3 In a large nonstick skillet, cook fish in oil over medium heat until cooked through, about 6 minutes per side.

4 Meanwhile, in a medium bowl, mix together the tomato sauce, spinach, and garlic. Stir to mix well. Pour evenly over fish.

5 Cover and cook, 5 or 6 minutes, to combine flavors. Add additional salt and pepper, if desired.

6 Arrange the pasta on a serving platter. Top with fish and then the tomato-spinach mixture. Sprinkle Parmesan cheese over all.

PERCH MEDITERRANEAN STYLE

This fast and flavorful fish dinner features perch, but you can substitute any mild white fish such as flounder, sole, halibut, or turbot. If your fish filets are thick, they will need the longer cooking time.

1 1/2 cups uncooked penne pasta or other similar pasta shape

1 cup fat-free low-sodium or regular chicken broth

1 8-oz can low-sodium or regular tomato sauce

2 Tbsp olive oil, divided

1 large green bell pepper, seeded and chopped

1/4 cup onion, chopped

1/2 cup dry-packed sun-dried tomatoes, diced

1 tsp minced garlic

1 tsp dried basil leaves

1 lb fresh or frozen (thawed) filets of perch or other lean white fish

Salt and pepper to taste

1 1/2 Tbsp grated Parmesan cheese

PREP TIME: 18 MINUTES

SERVINGS: 4

SERVING SIZE: 1 CUP PASTA AND SAUCE, 4 OZ FISH

Exchanges
1 1/2 Starch
2 Vegetable
3 Very Lean Meat
1 1/2 Fat

Calories 340
   Calories from Fat 81
Total Fat . . . . .9 g
   Saturated Fat . . . . .2 g
Cholesterol . . . . .62 mg
Sodium . . . . .288 mg
Total Carbohydrate . . . .34 g
   Dietary Fiber . . . . .4 g
   Sugars . . . . .9 g
Protein . . . . .30 g

1 Cook the pasta according to package directions. Rinse and drain. Transfer to a large bowl, and reserve.

2 Meanwhile, in a large skillet, combine the broth, tomato sauce, 1 tablespoon of the oil, green pepper, onion, tomatoes, garlic, and basil. Stir to mix well. Bring to a boil. Reduce heat and cook, uncovered, over low heat, 6 to 8 minutes, stirring frequently, until the onions are very tender and sauce has cooked down somewhat.

3 Remove the vegetables and all but about 3 tablespoons of liquid from the skillet. Transfer to bowl with pasta, and stir to mix.

4 Sprinkle fish with salt and pepper. Add remaining oil to pan. In batches, if necessary, cook the fish in the remaining liquid in skillet over medium heat, until cooked through, about 2 to 5 minutes per side, depending on thickness.

5 Arrange the vegetables and pasta on a serving platter. Arrange fish over vegetables and pasta. Sprinkle Parmesan cheese over all.

TILAPIA WITH OLIVES AND ARTICHOKES

"Here's an easy fish dinner, served Mediterranean style, over pasta. The recipe calls for tilapia, but you can substitute any mild white fish such as flounder, halibut, or turbot. Since you may find a wide variation in the thickness of fish filets, you may need to lengthen or shorten the cooking time."

3/4 cup fat-free low-sodium or regular chicken broth

2 Tbsp olive oil

1/2 cup chopped onion

1 tsp minced garlic

1 tsp dried basil leaves

1/2 tsp dried thyme leaves

Salt and pepper to taste (optional)

1 lb fresh or frozen (thawed) filets of tilapia

1 14 1/2-oz can artichoke heart quarters, coarse outer leaves removed

10 to 12 oil-cured black olives

1/3 cup crumbled feta cheese

4 oz (about 1 1/4 cups) spaghetti or other pasta shape, cooked according to package directions

PREP TIME: 15 MINUTES

SERVINGS: 4

SERVING SIZE: 1 CUP VEGETABLES AND FISH, PLUS 1 OZ PASTA

Exchanges
1 1/2 Starch
1 Vegetable
3 Very Lean Meat
2 Fat

Calories	.335
Calories from Fat	.103
Total Fat	.11 g
Saturated Fat	.3 g
Cholesterol	.67 mg
Sodium	.575 mg
Total Carbohydrate	.29 g
Dietary Fiber	.2 g
Sugars	.4 g
Protein	.28 g

1 In a large, nonstick skillet over medium heat, combine broth, oil, onion, garlic, basil, and thyme. Stir to mix well. Bring to a boil. Reduce the heat, and simmer, uncovered, 6 to 8 minutes, stirring frequently, until onions are very tender and sauce has cooked down somewhat.

2 Meanwhile, sprinkle salt and pepper on fish, if desired. Push the onions to the side of the skillet. In batches, if necessary, cook the fish in the broth mixture, over medium heat until white on one side. Turn with a spatula. Add artichoke hearts and olives to pan. Cover and cook over medium-high heat 6 to 8 minutes longer until the fish is cooked through. Sprinkle the cheese over all. Cook, uncovered, an additional 1 or 2 minutes.

3 Arrange the pasta on a serving platter. Arrange fish mixture over pasta.

Tuna, Tomatoes, and Greens over Pasta

With a couple cans of tuna and diced tomatoes in the cupboard, and a head of escarole or curly endive in the refrigerator, you can get a tasty family supper on the table in a jiffy.

1 large head (about 1 lb) escarole or curly endive

1 Tbsp olive oil

1 small onion, chopped

1 large clove garlic, peeled and minced

2 14 1/2-oz cans diced tomatoes

1/8 tsp dried hot red pepper flakes

   Black pepper to taste (optional)

2 6-oz cans water-packed white albacore tuna, very well drained

2 Tbsp coarsely chopped pitted Kalamata or other flavorful black olives (optional)

6 oz (about 1 3/4 cups) rotini or other medium corkscrew-shaped pasta, cooked according to package directions

PREP TIME: 20 MINUTES

SERVINGS: 5

SERVING SIZE: 1 CUP SAUCE, PLUS GENEROUS 1 OZ (2/3 CUP) PASTA

Exchanges
1 1/2 Starch
3 Vegetable
2 Very Lean Meat
1/2 Fat

Calories 273
    Calories from Fat 35
Total Fat . . . . .4 g
    Saturated Fat . . . . . . .1 g
Cholesterol . . . . .17 mg
Sodium . . . . .562 mg
Total Carbohydrate . . . .37 g
    Dietary Fiber . . . . .5 g
    Sugars . . . . .9 g
Protein . . . . .22 g

1 Trim off and discard the root end and the tough or dry outer leaves from the escarole (or endive). Thoroughly rinse the leaves in a colander under running water. Discard any tough stalk ends. Tear the leaves into small (1-inch) pieces; ready enough to yield 5 lightly packed cups. Thoroughly rinse the leaves again; let stand until well drained.

2 In a 12-inch nonstick skillet, combine the oil and onion over medium-high heat and cook, stirring frequently, until the onion is limp and beginning to brown, about 3 minutes. Add the garlic and cook, stirring, 2 minutes longer.

3 Stir in the tomatoes, escarole (or endive) leaves, red pepper flakes, and black pepper (if using); the leaves will overfill the skillet at first. Bring the mixture to a boil, stirring, until the leaves cook down and are covered with the tomato mixture. Adjust the heat so the mixture boils gently. Cover and cook, stirring occasionally, until the leaves are tender and the flavors are well blended, about 6 minutes longer.

4 Fold in the tuna and olives (if using), breaking up any very large chunks of tuna but leaving the small chunks intact. Heat until piping hot. Serve over the pasta.

BASIL-CHIVE PESTO AND PASTA

" If you've enjoyed pesto and pasta in fancy Italian restaurants, you'll like this homemade version even more. We've toasted the pine nuts because taking this step significantly increases their flavor. "

PESTO

> 3 *Tbsp pine nuts (about 1 oz)*
>
> 2 *tsp minced garlic*
>
> 1 1/2 *cups packed fresh basil leaves*
>
> 1/3 *cup packed chopped fresh chives or green onions*
>
> 1/4 *cup grated Parmesan cheese*
>
> 1 *Tbsp lemon juice*
>
> 1/4 *tsp salt, or more to taste*
>
> 1/3 *cup extra-virgin olive oil*

PASTA

> 1 *lb (about 4 cups) cooked pasta such as vermicelli or spaghetti, cooked according to package directions*

PREP TIME: 15 MINUTES

SERVINGS: 8

SERVING SIZE: 2 TBSP, PLUS 2 OZ PASTA OR 1/8 RECIPE

Exchanges
3 Starch
2 Fat

Calories 324
   Calories from Fat . . .109
Total Fat . . . . .12 g
   Saturated Fat . . . . .3 g
Cholesterol . . . . .4 mg
Sodium . . . . .142 mg
Total Carbohydrate . . . .44 g
   Dietary Fiber . . . . .2 g
   Sugars . . . . .3 g
Protein . . . . .10 g

1 Spread the nuts in a small, nonstick skillet. Cook over medium-high heat, stirring constantly, until the nuts begin to turn brown and smell toasted, about 3 to 4 minutes. Immediately transfer to a plate, and cool slightly.

2 Combine the nuts, garlic, basil, chives, cheese, lemon juice, and salt in a food processor container. Process until finely minced. With the processor on, slowly pour the oil through the feed tube; process until well blended, stopping and scraping down the sides of the container once or twice. Transfer to a small bowl.

3 To serve, toss individual servings of pesto with pasta. Pesto will keep tightly sealed in the refrigerator for 2 to 3 days or can be frozen for later use.

Vegetarian Spaghetti Sauce over Pasta

"You won't miss the meat in this hearty pasta sauce. Be sure to use high-protein pasta in the recipe."

1 large onion, chopped

1 tsp minced garlic

2 Tbsp olive oil

2 15-oz cans low-sodium or regular tomato sauce

1/2 large green bell pepper, seeded and chopped

2 cups diced zucchini

1 Tbsp Italian seasoning

1 large bay leaf

1/4 tsp ground black pepper

Salt to taste (optional)

1 to 2 tsp sugar, or to taste (optional)

8 oz (about 2 cups) thin spaghetti, cooked according to package directions

1/4 cup Parmesan cheese

PREP TIME: 15 MINUTES

SERVINGS: 4

SERVING SIZE: 1 CUP, PLUS 2 OZ PASTA

Exchanges
3 Starch
3 Vegetable
1 1/2 Fat

Calories 383
    Calories from Fat 86
Total Fat . . . . .10 g
    Saturated Fat . . . . . . .3 g
Cholesterol . . . . .8 mg
Sodium . . . . .185 mg
Total Carbohydrate . . . .61 g
    Dietary Fiber . . . . . . .5 g
    Sugars . . . . .17 g
Protein . . . . .14 g

1 In a Dutch oven or similar large pot, combine the onion, garlic, and oil. Cook over medium heat, stirring frequently, 5 or 6 minutes or until the onion is soft.

2 Add the tomato sauce, green pepper, zucchini, Italian seasoning, bay leaf, and pepper. Add salt to taste, if desired. If the tomatoes seem very acidic, add 2 teaspoons of sugar or to taste.

3 Bring to a boil. Cover, reduce the heat, and simmer 35 to 40 minutes, stirring occasionally, or until the vegetables are tender and the flavors are well blended. Remove and discard the bay leaf.

4 Arrange individual servings of spaghetti on dinner plates. Top each serving with sauce, then with 1 tablespoon of Parmesan cheese.

FRESH SPINACH, MUSHROOM, AND WHITE BEAN SAUCE OVER PASTA

Fresh, pre-washed, ready-to-use spinach is widely available in supermarkets and is delicious in this recipe. If possible, buy baby spinach—it's so tender you can eat the stems. You can use rigatoni, ziti, or even macaroni if that's what you have in the cupboard.

1 6- to 8-oz package fresh, ready-to-use baby leaf spinach

1 1/2 tsp olive oil

2 1/2 cups sliced fresh mushrooms

1 medium onion, chopped

1 large clove garlic, peeled and minced

1 cup fat-free reduced-sodium or regular chicken broth, plus more if needed

1 1/4 cups canned cannellini or great northern beans, rinsed and well drained

1/3 cup chopped fresh basil leaves or 2 Tbsp dried basil leaves

2 Tbsp commercially prepared basil pesto

1/4 tsp black pepper, or to taste

1/8 tsp salt (optional)

4 oz rotini or similar corkscrew-shaped pasta, cooked according to package directions (or use 2 cups leftover rotini pasta)

2 Tbsp grated Parmesan cheese

PREP TIME: 20 MINUTES

SERVINGS: 4

SERVING SIZE: 1 CUP SAUCE AND 1/2 CUP PASTA

Exchanges
2 Starch
2 1/2 Vegetable
1 1/2 Fat

Calories 291
   Calories from Fat 63
Total Fat . . . . .7 g
   Saturated Fat . . . . .2 g
Cholesterol . . . . .5 mg
Sodium . . . . .353 mg
Total Carbohydrate . . . .42 g
   Dietary Fiber . . . . . . .7 g
   Sugars . . . . .5 g
Protein . . . . .15 g

1 Transfer the spinach to a cutting board and chop finely; set aside.

2 In a 12-inch nonstick skillet, heat the oil to hot but not smoking over high heat. Add the mushrooms and onion. Adjust the heat so the vegetables cook rapidly but do not burn. Cook, stirring, until the vegetables are browned, about 5 minutes.

3 Stir in the garlic and continue cooking 1 minute longer. Stir in the broth, spinach, beans, basil, pesto, and pepper.

4 Adjust the heat so the mixture simmers, and cook, uncovered and stirring occasionally, for 2 to 4 minutes or until the spinach is tender.

5 Taste and add the salt, if desired. If necessary, thin the sauce with a little more chicken broth. Serve the sauce over the pasta and sprinkle the Parmesan cheese over the top.

Handy Tip

For a vegetarian dish, substitute vegetable broth for the chicken broth called for.

Hot from the
Oven and Broiler

BAKED HERBED CHICKEN AND VEGETABLES

"Aromatic and easy, this dinner requires no attention once it's slipped into the oven for baking."

2 1/2 Tbsp olive oil, divided

1 1/2 Tbsp all-purpose white flour

1 1/2 tsp chili powder

1 tsp paprika

1 tsp dried dillweed

1/2 tsp garlic salt

4 4-oz boneless, skinless chicken breast halves

1 large red bliss or other thin-skinned potato, cut into 1/3-inch cubes

2 large carrots, cut crosswise into 1/4-inch slices

2 medium turnips, peeled and cut into 1/3-inch cubes

1 medium celery stalk, cut crosswise into 1/4-inch slices

1 large onion, cut into eighths

1/8 tsp black pepper

PREP TIME: 20 MINUTES

SERVINGS: 4

SERVING SIZE: 1 CHICKEN BREAST, PLUS GENEROUS 3/4 CUP VEGETABLES

Exchanges
1 1/2 Starch
1 Vegetable
3 Very Lean Meat
1 1/2 Fat

Calories 327
  Calories from Fat 99
Total Fat . . . . .11 g
  Saturated Fat . . . . .3 g
Cholesterol . . . . .68 mg
Sodium . . . . .309 mg
Total Carbohydrate . . . .29 g
  Dietary Fiber . . . . .6 g
  Sugars . . . . .11 g
Protein . . . . .29 g

1 Preheat the oven to 425 degrees. Drizzle 1 1/2 tablespoons olive oil into a flat 9- × 13-inch baking dish, or similar-sized oven-proof dish.

2 In a sturdy paper or plastic bag, combine the flour, chili powder, paprika, dillweed, and garlic salt. Close the bag and shake well to blend. Pat the chicken breasts dry with paper towels. Add the chicken to the bag, close tightly, and shake until well coated on all sides with the seasoning. Holding the chicken pieces top side down, dip them into the oil in the baking dish until the surface is coated; then turn the pieces right side up in the dish. Reserve any leftover seasoning mixture.

3 In a large bowl, combine the potato, carrots, turnips, celery, onion, black pepper, and 1 teaspoon of the leftover seasoning mixture with 1 tablespoon oil, stirring well. Arrange the vegetables around the chicken, adjusting the chicken pieces so they are exposed to the heat rather than being buried under the vegetables. Sprinkle any leftover seasoning mixture over the chicken and vegetables.

4 Bake on the center oven rack for 30 to 40 minutes, or until the chicken is cooked through and the vegetables are tender when tested with a fork.

ARROZ CON POLLO

This is a lightened-up version of Arroz con Pollo, or Rice with Chicken, a popular dish in a number of Latin American countries. Our convenient, very tempting version is started on the burner, then slipped into the oven for fuss-free baking. If you like, the dish can be prepared and baked several days in advance, then returned to the oven for reheating just before serving time.

1 Tbsp olive oil

4 4-oz boneless, skinless chicken breast halves, trimmed of fat

1/4 tsp salt, divided

1/4 tsp black pepper, divided

1 large onion, chopped

1 small green bell pepper, seeded and cut into 1/2-inch chunks

1 large celery stalk, coarsely chopped

1 small clove garlic, peeled and minced

1 large tomato, peeled and chopped

1 1/4 tsp sweet or spicy paprika

1/4 tsp ground allspice

2/3 cup long-grain white rice

1 1/2 cups fat-free low-sodium or regular chicken broth

2 Tbsp sliced pimiento-stuffed green olives

PREP TIME: 25 MINUTES

SERVINGS: 4

SERVING SIZE: 1 CHICKEN BREAST HALF, PLUS 1 CUP RICE WITH VEGETABLES

Exchanges
1 1/2 Starch
2 Vegetable
3 Very Lean Meat
1 Fat

Calories 331
    Calories from Fat 64
Total Fat . . . . .7 g
    Saturated Fat . . . . .2 g
Cholesterol . . . . .68 mg
Sodium . . . . .510 mg
Total Carbohydrate . . . .36 g
    Dietary Fiber . . . . .3 g
    Sugars . . . . .7 g
Protein . . . . .30 g

1 Preheat the oven to 350 degrees. In a 4-quart Dutch oven or similar stove-top and oven-proof pot, heat 1 tablespoon oil to hot but not smoking over high heat. Add the chicken pieces; sprinkle them lightly with salt and pepper. Adjust the heat so the chicken pieces cook rapidly but don't burn; brown all over, turning frequently, about 7 to 9 minutes.

2 Remove the chicken and reserve. Add the onion, bell pepper, and celery to the pot. Cook, scraping the pot bottom, until the onion is translucent, about 5 minutes. Stir in the garlic; cook 30 seconds longer.

3 Stir in the tomato, paprika, allspice, rice, broth, olives, and the remaining salt and pepper. Bring to a simmer. Return the chicken pieces to the pot. Cover the pot tightly.

4 Transfer to the oven. Cook 15 to 20 minutes longer, or until the chicken and rice are just tender when tested with a fork.

CHICKEN AND VEGETABLES MARRAKESH

Ground coriander, cinnamon, and raisins add a mild yet pleasingly exotic taste to this simple chicken stew.

1 1/2 *Tbsp olive oil*

1 *lb skinless, boneless chicken breast, cut into 1-inch cubes*

2 *tsp ground coriander*

1/4 *tsp ground cinnamon*

Scant 1/2 *tsp salt, or to taste*

1/4 *tsp ground black pepper*

3 *medium carrots, peeled and cut crosswise into 1/4 inch–thick slices*

2 *medium onions, very coarsely chopped*

1 *large green bell pepper, cored, seeded, and cut into 3/4-inch chunks*

1/4 *cup fat-free low-sodium or regular chicken broth*

1/4 *cup dark or golden raisins*

PREP TIME: 20 MINUTES

SERVINGS: 4

SERVING SIZE: 1 1/2 CUPS

Exchanges
3 Very Lean Meat
1/2 Fruit
3 Vegetable
1 1/2 Fat

Calories 270
   Calories from Fat 70
Total Fat . . . . .8 g
   Saturated Fat . . . . .2 g
Cholesterol . . . . .68 mg
Sodium . . . . .407 mg
Total Carbohydrate . . . .23 g
   Dietary Fiber . . . . .4 g
   Sugars . . . . .15 g
Protein . . . . .28 g

1 Preheat the oven to 400 degrees.

2 Heat the oil to hot over medium-high heat in a 12-inch deep-sided stove-top and oven-proof casserole (or similar-size skillet with oven-proof handle). Add the chicken pieces and sprinkle on both sides with the coriander, cinnamon, salt, and pepper. Adjust the heat so the chicken cooks briskly but doesn't burn and brown the pieces, turning frequently, for 4 minutes.

3 Stir the carrots, onions, and green pepper into the casserole. Cook, stirring, until the vegetables are just heated through, 3 to 4 minutes longer. Add the broth and raisins; bring to a boil.

4 Transfer the casserole to the oven and bake uncovered on the center oven rack for 18 to 23 minutes, or until the chicken pieces and vegetables are tender when pierced in the thickest part with a fork. Add more salt and pepper to taste, if desired.

TURKEY (OR CHICKEN) AND DUMPLINGS

This is a very satisfying home-style recipe starts on the stovetop and finishes in the oven. If you don't have a deep-sided skillet that will go from burner to oven, transfer the turkey-vegetable mixture to a large baking dish just before topping with the dumplings.

2 tsp canola oil

3 medium carrots, peeled and chopped

3 medium celery stalks, coarsely diced

5 or 6 green onions, including tender tops, very coarsely diced

2 1/2 cups fat-free reduced-sodium chicken broth, divided

1 cup diced cauliflower florets

1 tsp dried marjoram leaves

2 bay leaves

1/4 tsp salt (optional)

1/8 to 1/4 tsp black pepper, to taste

2 1/2 Tbsp cornstarch

2 1/2 cups very coarsely diced roasted turkey (or chicken) white meat

DUMPLINGS

1 cup all-purpose white flour

1/4 tsp salt

Scant 1/2 tsp baking soda

2 Tbsp olive oil

2/3 cup nonfat milk combined with 1 Tbsp lemon juice

PREP TIME: 25 MINUTES

SERVINGS: 4

SERVING SIZE: GENEROUS 1 CUP TURKEY AND VEGETABLES, AND 2 DUMPLINGS

Exchanges
2 Vegetable
2 Starch
4 Lean Meat

Calories 415
    Calories from Fat 99
Total Fat . . . . .11 g
    Saturated Fat . . . . .1 g
Cholesterol . . . . .79 mg
Sodium . . . . .751 mg
Total Carbohydrate . . . .43 g
    Dietary Fiber . . . . .6 g
    Sugars . . . . .8 g
Protein . . . . .36 g

1 Preheat the oven to 425 degrees. In a 12-inch, deep-sided stove-top and oven-proof casserole (or a 12-inch deep-sided skillet with an oven-proof handle), combine the oil, carrots, celery, and green onions over medium-high heat. Cook, stirring, until the vegetables are lightly browned, about 5 minutes.

2 Stir in 2 cups broth, the cauliflower, marjoram, bay leaves, salt, and pepper. Bring to a boil; then adjust the heat so the mixture simmers for 5 minutes. Remove the bay leaves and discard. Taste and add more salt, if desired.

3 In a small bowl or cup, combine the remaining 1/2 cup broth with the cornstarch, stirring until well blended. Stir the cornstarch-broth mixture and the turkey meat into the vegetable mixture until thoroughly incorporated. Heat until hot; remove from the burner.

4 Ready the dumpling mixture: In a small, deep bowl, thoroughly stir together the flour, salt, and baking soda. Stir in the oil, then stir in about 1/2 cup of the milk-lemon juice mixture. Add enough more of the milk-lemon juice mixture to yield a soft, moist dough; for tender dumplings stir only enough to mix the ingredients.

5 Using large spoons, drop the dough into 8 equal-size dumpling mounds, spacing them evenly over the turkey mixture. Transfer to the oven. Bake, uncovered, in the upper third of the oven for 15 to 20 minutes, or until the dumplings are puffy and browned and a toothpick inserted in a center dumpling comes out clean.

TURKEY MARENGO

This hearty stew starts on the stove top, then goes in the oven for baking. Traditionally, the classic French dish called "Marengo" is prepared with veal, but turkey breast meat, which is leaner, stands in beautifully. If you wish, the stew can be made ahead and then reheated for a completely fuss-free meal.

1 1/4 lb boneless, skinless turkey breast meat, cut into 1-inch cubes

2 Tbsp all-purpose white flour

1/2 tsp salt

1/4 to 1/2 tsp black pepper, to taste

1/2 tsp paprika

3 Tbsp corn oil or canola oil, divided

2 medium onions, chopped

1 large celery stalk, chopped

1 1/2 cups coarsely sliced carrots

1 1/2 cups button mushrooms or very coarsely sliced regular mushrooms

1/3 cup fat-free low-sodium or regular chicken broth

3/4 tsp dried tarragon leaves

3/4 tsp dried thyme leaves

1 14 1/2-oz can diced tomatoes

1/4 cup moderately dry white table wine or orange juice, if preferred

PREP TIME: 25 MINUTES

SERVINGS: 6

SERVING SIZE: 1 CUP

Exchanges
3 Very Lean Meat
3 Vegetable
1 Fat

Calories 229
    Calories from Fat 72
Total Fat . . . . .8 g
    Saturated Fat . . . . .0 g
Cholesterol . . . . .61 mg
Sodium . . . . .418 mg
Total Carbohydrate . . . .14 g
    Dietary Fiber . . . . .3 g
    Sugars . . . . .8 g
Protein . . . . .25 g

1 Preheat the oven to 375 degrees. Lightly pat the turkey cubes dry with paper towels. Combine the cubes in a large sturdy paper or plastic bag with the flour, salt, pepper, and paprika. Close the bag tightly. Shake until all the flour coats the cubes.

2 In a 12-inch, nonstick, deep-sided skillet with oven-proof handle (or similar nonstick stove-top and oven-proof casserole), heat 1 1/2 tablespoons oil to hot but not smoking over high heat. Add half the turkey cubes and brown, turning constantly and scraping the skillet bottom, about 4 minutes; adjust the heat so the cubes cook briskly but do not burn. Remove the cubes and any browned bits from the skillet and reserve. Heat the remaining oil to hot. Brown the remaining cubes, turning constantly and scraping up any browned bits. Reserve them with the first batch.

3 Add the onions, celery, carrots, and mushrooms to the skillet. Cook, stirring frequently, until the onions are limp and beginning to brown, about 5 minutes. (If necessary, adjust the heat to prevent the vegetables from burning.)

4 Stir the broth, tarragon, and thyme into the pot. Return the turkey and any juices to the pot. Stir in the tomatoes and wine (or juice). Let the mixture just return to a boil. Cover the pot tightly.

5 Transfer to the center rack of the oven. Cook, covered, 20 to 25 minutes longer, until the turkey and vegetables are tender when tested with a fork.

TAMALE PIE

"Here's a California classic that you make like a lasagna, layering filling and corn tortillas."

3/4 lb ground beef round

2 cups frozen onion and pepper stir-fry

1 tsp minced garlic

2 15-oz cans low-sodium or regular tomato sauce

1 15-oz can light red low-sodium or regular kidney beans, rinsed and drained

1 1/2 cups frozen corn kernels

1 Tbsp chili powder (or to taste)

1 tsp ground cumin

1/4 tsp salt (optional)

1/4 tsp black pepper

1 9-oz package 6-inch diameter corn tortillas

3/4 cup reduced-fat shredded cheddar cheese

PREP TIME: 18 MINUTES

SERVINGS: 7

SERVING SIZE: 1 CUP

Exchanges
2 1/2 Starch
1 Lean Meat
2 Vegetable

Calories 301
   Calories from Fat 51
Total Fat . . . . .6 g
   Saturated Fat . . . . .2 g
Cholesterol . . . . .33 mg
Sodium . . . . .227 mg
Total Carbohydrate . . . .44 g
   Dietary Fiber . . . . .8 g
   Sugars . . . . .10 g
Protein . . . . .21 g

1 Preheat oven to 350 degrees. In a 3-quart flame-proof, oven-proof casserole, combine the ground round, onions and peppers, and garlic. Cook over medium heat, stirring frequently, until the beef has changed color. Remove casserole from burner.

2 Add the tomato sauce, kidney beans, corn, chili powder, cumin, salt, if desired, and black pepper. Stir to mix well. Scoop out 6 cups of the mixture, and reserve in a medium bowl. Lay 1/3 of the tortillas over the mixture remaining in the casserole, overlapping and covering the entire surface. Add 2 cups of the reserved meat and bean mixture, spreading it out with the back of a large spoon. Lay another 1/3 of the tortillas over the mixture in the casserole, overlapping and covering the entire surface. Top with 2 cups of the meat and bean mixture. Top with the remaining tortillas and the remaining meat and bean mixture, spreading it out evenly over tortillas.

3 Bake uncovered for 45 to 50 minutes or until the sauce begins to bubble and flavors are well blended. Top with cheddar cheese, and bake an additional 2 or 3 minutes or until cheese melts.

ITALIAN STUFFED PEPPERS

"These stuffed peppers are like little mini-lasagnas—in a juicy pepper shell."

3 large green peppers, cut in half
    lengthwise, seeded and
    stems removed

1/2 lb lean ground beef

1 medium onion, chopped

1 15-oz can Italian-seasoned tomato
    sauce, divided

1 cup cooked small pasta, such as small
    elbows, prepared without added fat or
    salt

1/2 cup reduced-fat ricotta cheese

3/4 cup shredded fat-free mozzarella cheese

2 Tbsp grated Parmesan cheese

PREP TIME: 20 MINUTES

SERVINGS: 6

SERVING SIZE: 1 PEPPER
    HALF WITH STUFFING

Exchanges
1 Starch
1 Vegetable
2 Very Lean Meat

Calories 179
    Calories from Fat 27
Total Fat . . . . .3 g
    Saturated Fat . . . . . . .1 g
Cholesterol . . . . .29 mg
Sodium . . . . .546 mg
Total Carbohydrate . . . .20 g
    Dietary Fiber . . . . .4 g
    Sugars . . . . .6 g
Protein . . . . .18 g

1 Spray a 9 1/2- × 13-inch baking pan with nonstick spray. Set aside. Preheat oven to 350 degrees.

2 In a large pot, place the pepper halves in boiling water for 3 or 4 minutes until the peppers are partially cooked. Drain in a colander, and reserve in the baking dish.

3 In a large skillet, combine the ground beef and onion. Cook over medium heat, stirring frequently, until the beef is browned and the onion is softened, about 6 or 7 minutes. Drain fat off meat mixture. Stir in all but 1/2 cup of the tomato sauce. Remove from heat. Stir in the cooked pasta. Divide the meat mixture evenly among the pepper halves.

4 Spoon the ricotta over the meat mixture, dividing evenly. Sprinkle the mozzarella over the ricotta, dividing evenly. Top with the remaining tomato sauce, dividing evenly, then Parmesan cheese, dividing evenly.

5 Bake for 25 to 30 minutes on the center oven rack or until the mixture is cooked through and the flavors are well blended.

CHEESE AND RICE STUFFED PEPPERS

" These very tasty stuffed peppers are a good choice when you want a meatless meal. You can use leftover rice, or ready some quick-cooking rice to use in the filling. "

4 large (about 4 inch–long) green peppers, halved lengthwise and stems removed

1 6-oz package fresh, ready-to-use baby leaf spinach

1 1/2 cups shredded fat-free mozzarella cheese

1 1/4 cups 1 percent fat (not salt-free) cottage cheese

1 1/2 cups cooked brown or white rice

1/2 cup chopped fresh parsley leaves

3 Tbsp grated Parmesan cheese

1 tsp dried oregano leaves

1 tsp minced garlic

2 to 3 drops hot pepper sauce or a pinch of ground hot red pepper

1/2 cup no-salt-added or reduced-sodium tomato sauce

PREP TIME: 20 MINUTES

SERVINGS: 4

SERVING SIZE: 2 STUFFED PEPPER HALVES WITH SAUCE

Exchanges
2 Starch
1 Vegetable
3 Very Lean Meat

Calories 283
    Calories from Fat 27
Total Fat . . . . .3 g
    Saturated Fat . . . . .1 g
Cholesterol . . . . .14 mg
Sodium . . . . .707 mg
Total Carbohydrate . . . .35 g
    Dietary Fiber . . . . .7 g
    Sugars . . . . .9 g
Protein . . . . .29 g

1 Spray a 9 1/2- × 13-inch baking dish with nonstick spray. Set aside. Preheat the oven to 350 degrees.

2 In a large pot, place the pepper halves in boiling water, and boil for 6 minutes until the peppers are slightly tender when tested with a fork.

3 Place the spinach in a large colander set in the sink. Pour the peppers and boiling water over the spinach; the leaves will wilt. Drain the peppers and spinach well. Place the peppers, cut-side up, in the baking pan. Squeeze out the excess moisture from the spinach.

4 In a large bowl, stir together the mozzarella, cottage cheese, rice, parsley, Parmesan cheese, oregano, garlic, and hot pepper sauce or red pepper. Coarsely chop the spinach and stir it into the filling.

5 Put the cheese mixture into the pepper halves, dividing evenly.

6 Bake for 20 to 25 minutes on the center oven rack or until the filling is cooked through and the peppers are tender when pierced with a fork. Remove from oven, and top with tomato sauce, dividing it evenly. Bake an additional 4 or 5 minutes.

SHEPHERD'S PIE

Traditionally, Shepherd's Pie is topped with potatoes. Here's an easy version with a biscuit topping. Frozen vegetables and refrigerator biscuits speed the preparation of this tasty dinner.

1 lb beef round, trimmed of all fat

2 Tbsp olive oil, divided

1 cup chopped onion

1 tsp minced garlic

1 1/4 cups defatted beef broth

1 8-oz can low-sodium or regular tomato sauce

2 cups frozen carrots and peas

2 cups frozen green bean pieces

2 large bay leaves

1 tsp dried thyme leaves

1/2 tsp dried marjoram leaves

1/4 tsp dry mustard

1/4 tsp black pepper

1/4 tsp salt, or to taste (optional)

1 6-oz package low-fat or regular refrigerator biscuits

PREP TIME: 20 MINUTES

SERVINGS: 5

SERVING SIZE: 1 GENEROUS CUP, PLUS 1 WHOLE BISCUIT

Exchanges
2 1/2 Starch
2 Vegetable
1/2 Fat
2 Lean Meat

Calories 313
  Calories from Fat 97
Total Fat . . . . .11 g
  Saturated Fat . . . . .3 g
Cholesterol . . . . .47 mg
Sodium . . . . .783 mg
Total Carbohydrate . . . .31 g
  Dietary Fiber . . . . .5 g
  Sugars . . . . .12 g
Protein . . . . .21 g

1 Preheat the oven to 350 degrees. Cut meat into very thin 2 inch–long diagonal strips.

2 In 3-quart flame-proof, oven-proof casserole, or a small Dutch oven, brown the meat in 1 tablespoon of oil over medium-high heat, stirring frequently, about 6 or 7 minutes. With a slotted spoon, remove the meat to a medium bowl and reserve.

3 In the casserole, combine the onion, garlic, and remaining oil. Cook over medium heat, stirring, 6 or 7 minutes, or until onion is tender. If vegetables begin to stick, add a bit of the broth.

4 Return the meat to the casserole. Stir in the beef broth and tomato sauce. Stir in the carrots and peas and green beans along with the bay leaves, thyme, marjoram, mustard, pepper, and salt, if desired. Stir to mix well. Bake, covered, for 1 hour, or until the meat is tender.

5 Remove the casserole from the oven. Remove the bay leaves. Turn up the oven temperature to 400 degrees. Open the biscuit package, and separate the biscuits. With a sharp knife, carefully split each biscuit in half to form two rounds. When all the biscuits are cut, lay them over top of the meat mixture, squeezing them together if necessary. Bake, uncovered, 11 to 12 minutes or until the biscuits begin to brown and are cooked through.

TANGY POT ROAST WITH WINTER VEGETABLES

Here's a savory winter dinner when you have a little extra time to let a roast simmer in the oven. Leftovers can be quickly reheated in the microwave. Incidentally, this dish works best if you purchase a long, thin roast rather than a fatter one. The meat will cook more quickly, and you'll find slicing easier, too.

1 2-lb beef round roast, trimmed of all fat
  Salt and pepper to taste
3 Tbsp olive oil
1 cup fat-free low-sodium or regular chicken broth
1 15-oz can low-sodium or regular tomato sauce
1 Tbsp sugar
1 Tbsp red wine vinegar
1 1/2 tsp Dijon-style mustard
1 tsp minced garlic
1 1/2 tsp dried thyme leaves
1 bay leaf
15 baby carrots
1 cup peeled and cubed rutabaga
2 celery stalks, sliced
3 large boiling potatoes, peeled and cut into large pieces

PREP TIME: 20 MINUTES

SERVINGS: 8

SERVING SIZE: 2 SLICES OF MEAT, PLUS 1 CUP VEGETABLES AND SAUCE

Exchanges
1 Starch
3 Lean Meat
1 Vegetable

Calories 266
  Calories from Fat 76
Total Fat . . . . .8 g
  Saturated Fat . . . . .2 g
Cholesterol . . . . .52 mg
Sodium . . . . .170 mg
Total Carbohydrate . . . .23 g
  Dietary Fiber . . . . .3 g
  Sugars . . . . .8 g
Protein . . . . .24 g

1 Preheat oven to 350 degrees. Sprinkle roast with salt, if desired, and pepper. In a large oven-proof Dutch oven or similar pot over medium-high heat, brown the meat in the oil, turning to brown all sides. If the meat begins to stick to the bottom of the pot, reduce the heat. Drain off the oil.

2 Add the broth. Scrape up any browned bits of meat from the pot bottom. Add the tomato sauce, sugar, vinegar, mustard, garlic, thyme, and bay leaf. Stir to mix well. Stir in the carrots, rutabaga, celery, and potatoes, stirring them down into the sauce. Spoon some sauce over the meat.

3 Cover and cook in the center of the oven for 1 1/2 to 2 hours, checking occasionally to make sure the sauce is not sticking to the bottom of the pot, until the roast is tender.

4 Remove and discard the bay leaf. Add additional salt and pepper to taste, if desired. Slice the roast and arrange on serving platter; surround with vegetables. Pour some sauce over the meat, and pass additional sauce. Leftover roast will keep in the refrigerator for 3 or 4 days.

BRAISED BEEF AND VEGETABLES DINNER

The secret to the succulence of this hearty dinner is in the oven braising. It brings out both the flavor of the beef and the vegetables. If desired, make the dinner several days ahead and reheat it at serving time.

1 1/2 Tbsp corn oil or canola oil, divided

1 1/4 lb lean beef top round, trimmed of fat and cut into scant 1-inch cubes

1 1/4 cups low-sodium or regular beef broth, divided

1 tsp dried thyme leaves

1/2 tsp salt, divided

2 cups 1 1/4-inch chunks unpeeled red bliss potatoes

2 medium onions, peeled and quartered

2 medium celery stalks, cut into 1-inch pieces

1 3/4 cups peeled baby carrots

1 3/4 cups whole green beans, ends trimmed

Black pepper to taste

PREP TIME: 20 MINUTES

SERVINGS: 5

SERVING SIZE: 1 1/2 CUPS

Exchanges
1/2 Starch
3 Vegetable
3 Lean Meat

Calories 270
   Calories from Fat 74
Total Fat . . . . .8 g
   Saturated Fat . . . . .1 g
Cholesterol . . . . .52 mg
Sodium . . . . .431 mg
Total Carbohydrate . . . .24 g
   Dietary Fiber . . . . .5 g
   Sugars . . . . .8 g
Protein . . . . .25 g

1 Preheat the oven to 400 degrees. In a 4-quart Dutch oven or similar stove-top and oven-proof pot, heat 1/2 tablespoon oil to hot but not smoking over high heat. Add half the beef cubes and brown, turning frequently. Remove the cubes and reserve. Heat 1/2 tablespoon more oil to hot. Brown the remaining cubes, turning.

2 Return all the beef to the pot. Add 1 tablespoon broth, the thyme, and 1/4 teaspoon salt, stirring and scraping the pot bottom until well mixed; cook briskly for 9 or 10 minutes longer, adding a little more broth if needed to prevent the pot from boiling dry.

3 Stir the potatoes, onion, celery, carrots, and green beans into the pot. Drizzle the remaining 1/2 tablespoon olive oil over top; stir until the vegetables are well coated. Add the remaining broth. Sprinkle with the remaining salt. Cover the pot tightly.

4 Transfer to the oven and cook 45 to 55 minutes longer, until the beef and vegetables are tender when tested with a fork. Add black pepper to taste, if desired.

BEEF AND MUSHROOM GOULASH

Start this hearty goulash by browning the beef and mushrooms on top of the stove. Then, transfer the goulash to the oven and let it bake for about 45 minutes until the beef is tender and succulent.

1 1/2 Tbsp corn oil or canola oil, divided

1 lb lean top round steak, trimmed of fat and cut into 3/4-inch cubes

Salt and black pepper to taste

3 1/2 cups coarsely sliced mushrooms

1 large onion, chopped

2 large celery stalks, chopped

1/2 tsp dried thyme leaves

2 Tbsp all-purpose white flour

1 cup low-sodium or regular beef broth

3 Tbsp ketchup

2 tsp Worcestershire sauce

1 Tbsp sweet Hungarian paprika

3 Tbsp reduced-fat sour cream

2 cups hot cooked wide egg noodles for serving

PREP TIME: 30 MINUTES

SERVINGS: 4

SERVING SIZE: 1 CUP GOULASH, PLUS 1/2 CUP NOODLES

Exchanges
1 1/2 Starch
3 Vegetable
3 Lean Meat
1/2 Fat

Calories 372
  Calories from Fat . . .118
Total Fat . . . . .13 g
  Saturated Fat . . . . .2 g
Cholesterol . . . . .88 mg
Sodium . . . . .353 mg
Total Carbohydrate . . . .37 g
  Dietary Fiber . . . . .4 g
  Sugars . . . . .9 g
Protein . . . . .27 g

1 Preheat the oven to 400 degrees. In a 4-quart Dutch oven or similar stove-top and oven-proof pot, heat 1/2 tablespoon oil to hot but not smoking over high heat.

2 Add half the beef cubes. Sprinkle lightly with salt and pepper and brown, turning frequently. Adjust the heat so the beef cooks rapidly but does not burn. Cook, stirring, until the cubes are nicely browned, about 3 minutes. Remove the cubes and reserve. Heat 1/2 tablespoon more oil to hot. Add the remaining beef cubes. Season lightly with salt and pepper. Repeat the browning process. Remove the cubes and reserve.

3 Heat the remaining 1/2 tablespoon oil to hot in the Dutch oven. Stir in the mushrooms, onion, celery, and thyme. Cook, stirring, until the mushrooms release their juices and are lightly browned, about 5 minutes.

4 Return the beef to the Dutch oven. Add the flour and cook, stirring, for about 1 1/2 minutes longer.

5 Vigorously stir in the broth, ketchup, Worcestershire sauce, and paprika until smoothly incorporated. Let return to a boil over high heat.

6 Cover the pot tightly and transfer to the oven. Cook for 40 to 50 minutes, or until the beef is just tender when tested with a fork.

7 Remove from the heat; stir in the sour cream until smoothly incorporated. Serve the goulash over noodles.

BEEF AND SPINACH LASAGNA

Lasagna makes a great main dish for a crowd. But it's a bit time-consuming to put together. To streamline the process, we've made this lasagna with "no-boil" noodles. (The product is sometimes called "oven-ready" pasta.) Since the noodles are shorter than conventional lasagna noodles, lay them across the pan rather than lengthwise.

1/2 lb extra-lean ground beef

1 large onion, diced (1 1/4 cups)

1 tsp minced garlic

1 28-oz jar tomato and herb pasta sauce

1 15-oz can no-salt-added or regular tomato sauce

2 1/2 cups packed, fresh, ready-to-use baby spinach leaves, chopped

1 tsp dried thyme leaves

1/2 tsp dried oregano leaves

1/4 tsp ground black pepper

1/2 tsp salt (optional)

9 no-boil (oven-ready) lasagna noodles

1 cup nonfat ricotta cheese

1 8-oz package shredded fat-free mozzarella cheese, divided

PREP TIME: 20 MINUTES

SERVINGS: 9

SERVING SIZE: 1/9 LASAGNA

Exchanges
2 Vegetable
1 Starch
1 Skim Milk
1 Very Lean Meat

Calories 259
   Calories from Fat 27
Total Fat . . . . .3 g
   Saturated Fat . . . . .1 g
Cholesterol . . . . .22 mg
Sodium . . . . .563 mg
Total Carbohydrate . . . .37 g
   Dietary Fiber . . . . .5 g
   Sugars . . . . .13 g
Protein . . . . .21 g

1 Preheat the oven to 350 degrees.

2 In a medium pot over medium heat, cook the ground beef, onion, and garlic, stirring occasionally, until the beef is brown and the onion is soft.

3 Add the pasta sauce and tomato sauce, spinach, thyme, oregano, and pepper. Bring to a boil. Reduce the heat and simmer about 10 minutes, or until the flavors are blended and the sauce is cooked down slightly. Taste and add salt, if desired.

4 Spread a thin layer, about 1 3/4 cups, of the sauce in the bottom of a 9 1/2- × 13-inch pan. Arrange a layer of 3 noodles over the sauce. Top with the ricotta, spreading it out evenly with the back of a spoon. Sprinkle with 1/3 of the mozzarella. Add 1/3 of the remaining sauce.

5 Add another layer of 3 noodles. Add 1/3 of the remaining sauce and 1/3 of the mozzarella. Finish with a final layer of noodles, carefully covering them with the remaining sauce. Reserve the remaining mozzarella.

6 Tightly cover the dish with foil. Bake on the middle rack for 30 minutes. Uncover and bake 10 minutes longer, or until noodles in the center are tender when pierced with a fork. Sprinkle with the remaining mozzarella cheese during the last 5 minutes of baking. Let the lasagna stand for 5 to 10 minutes before cutting into 9 portions.

MEDITERRANEAN-STYLE BAKED FLOUNDER WITH VEGETABLE-RICE PILAF

"Black olives, fresh tomatoes, bell peppers, and zucchini lend both rich flavor and color to the pilaf. It complements the mild, tender fish well."

1 1/2 Tbsp olive oil, divided

1 medium zucchini, coarsely diced

1 small red or green bell pepper, seeded and finely chopped

2 or 3 green onions, trimmed and coarsely chopped

1 large tomato, peeled and coarsely chopped

3 Tbsp chopped pitted black Nicoise or Kalamata olives

1/2 tsp dried oregano leaves

1/2 cup fat-free low-sodium or regular chicken broth

1/2 cup quick-cooking white rice

1 lb fresh boneless, skinless flounder filets, or 1 lb package frozen (thawed) boneless, skinless flounder filets, or other mild white-fish filets

Salt and black pepper to taste (optional)

PREP TIME: 20 MINUTES

SERVINGS: 4

SERVING SIZE: 4 OZ FISH, PLUS 3/4 CUP PILAF

Exchanges
1/2 Starch
1 Vegetable
3 Very Lean Meat
1 Fat

Calories 224
    Calories from Fat 61
Total Fat . . . . .7 g
    Saturated Fat . . . . .1 g
Cholesterol . . . . .59 mg
Sodium . . . . .219 mg
Total Carbohydrate . . . .16 g
    Dietary Fiber . . . . .2 g
    Sugars . . . . .3 g
Protein . . . . .24 g

1 Preheat the oven to 425 degrees.

2 In a 12-inch (or similar) round stove-top and oven-proof casserole or baking dish, combine 1 tablespoon oil, zucchini, bell pepper, and green onions over medium-high heat. Cook, stirring, until the zucchini begins to brown, about 5 minutes.

3 Stir in the tomato, olives, and oregano; cook 2 minutes longer.

4 Stir the broth and rice into the mixture. If the fish filets are very large, cut them up to yield 4 portions. Lay the fish filets over the top of the pilaf. Brush the fish with the remaining 1/2 tablespoon olive oil, then sprinkle with salt and pepper to taste.

5 Bake for 15 to 20 minutes, until the pilaf is tender and the fish flakes when tested in the thickest part with a fork.

SALMON BAKE

We're fans of salmon—both because we love the taste and because we know it's so nutritious. This recipe takes about the same time to prepare as salmon loaf, only when it's finished, we've got tasty baked open-faced salmon sandwiches. The food processor grates and shreds the vegetables in a snap.

4 1/4 slices low-calorie whole-wheat bread

1 14 1/2-oz can pink salmon, drained and skin removed

3 large egg whites plus 1 large egg

1/4 cup reduced-fat mayonnaise

1 Tbsp instant minced onions

1/2 tsp dried basil leaves

1/2 tsp dry mustard

1/4 tsp ground celery seed

1 celery stalk, grated or shredded

1 cup grated or shredded cauliflower florets

PREP TIME: 18 MINUTES

SERVINGS: 4

SERVING SIZE: 1/4 CASSEROLE

Exchanges
1/2 Starch
1 Vegetable
3 Lean Meat
1 Fat

Calories 276
    Calories from Fat . . .115
Total Fat . . . . .13 g
    Saturated Fat . . . . .1 g
Cholesterol . . . . .116 mg
Sodium . . . . .893 mg
Total Carbohydrate . . . .13 g
    Dietary Fiber . . . . .4 g
    Sugars . . . . .2 g
Protein . . . . .28 g

1 Preheat the oven to 350 degrees. Spray an 8- × 11-inch flat glass baking dish with nonstick cooking spray. Lightly toast the bread slices. Arrange the bread slices in baking dish bottom, cutting them to fit so that the bottom surface of the dish is covered. Set aside.

2 Place the salmon in a large bowl, and use a fork to flake it. Add the egg whites and egg and mayonnaise, and stir to combine well.

3 Stir in the onions, basil, mustard, and celery seed. Stir in the celery and cauliflower. Spread the mixture evenly over the bread.

4 Bake for 30 to 35 minutes until the eggs are set and the mixture begins to brown. Cut into squares with a knife and serve.

VERA CRUZ-STYLE FISH AND VEGETABLE BAKE

Onions, sweet peppers, green olives, capers, and aromatic spices enliven this regional Mexican fish dish. It starts on a burner, then finishes in the oven.

1 1/2 Tbsp olive oil

1 large onion, chopped

1 large red bell pepper, seeded and coarsely chopped

1 medium celery stalk, coarsely chopped

1 large clove garlic, peeled and minced

1 8-oz can low-sodium tomato sauce

1/2 cup fat-free low-sodium or regular chicken broth

1 tsp sweet or spicy paprika

1/2 tsp ground allspice

1/2 tsp dried oregano leaves

1/4 tsp black pepper, or to taste

3 Tbsp sliced pimiento-stuffed green olives

2 Tbsp capers

1 lb boneless, skinless cod, flounder, or other mild white fish filets

1/4 tsp salt to taste (optional)

2 cups hot cooked white or brown rice

PREP TIME: 20 MINUTES

SERVINGS: 4

SERVING SIZE: 4 OZ FISH FILET, PLUS GENEROUS 1/2 CUP VEGETABLES, PLUS 1/2 CUP RICE

Exchanges
1 1/2 Starch
2 Vegetable
2 Very Lean Meat
1 Fat

Calories	305
Calories from Fat	61
Total Fat	7 g
Saturated Fat	1 g
Cholesterol	48 mg
Sodium	242 mg
Total Carbohydrate	36 g
Dietary Fiber	7 g
Sugars	9 g
Protein	24 g

1 Preheat the oven to 350 degrees.

2 In a 12-inch or slightly larger stove-top and oven-proof casserole or skillet with an oven-safe handle, heat the oil to hot but not smoking over high heat. Add the onion, bell pepper, and celery to the pan. Cook, scraping the pot bottom, until the vegetables are lightly browned, about 5 or 6 minutes. Stir in the garlic; cook 30 seconds longer.

3 Stir in the tomato sauce, broth, paprika, allspice, oregano, pepper, olives, and capers. Bring to a simmer; cook 3 or 4 minutes to allow the flavors to blend.

4 If the fish pieces are large, cut them into 4 servings. Scoop up about a cup of the vegetable mixture and reserve. Lay the filets in the casserole. Spread the reserved vegetable mixture over the filets.

5 Transfer the casserole to the oven. Bake, uncovered, for 15 to 20 minutes, or until the fish just flakes when tested with a fork in the thickest part. Add salt to taste, if desired.

6 Serve the filets on a bed of rice with the vegetable mixture spooned over top.

Vegetable Frittata with Cheddar

Use a skillet that can go from the stovetop into the oven for this "crustless" vegetable pie. Or simply transfer the sauteed mixture from a skillet to a 10 inch–diameter, 2 inch–deep pie plate or similar size oven-proof flat round casserole before baking.

1 Tbsp olive oil

1 cup finely chopped onion

3/4 cup sliced mushrooms

1 cup plain whole-grain croutons or cubed day-old whole-grain bread (1/4-inch cubes)

1/8 tsp salt

1/2 cup well-drained and diced roasted red sweet peppers

2 large eggs

1 8-oz carton liquid egg substitute

1/4 cup reduced-fat milk

2/3 cup shredded, reduced-fat sharp cheddar cheese, divided

1 tsp prepared Dijon or regular yellow mustard

1/4 tsp ground black pepper

PREP TIME: 20 MINUTES

SERVINGS: 5

SERVING SIZE: 1/5 FRITTATA

Exchanges
1/2 Starch
2 Lean Meat
1/2 Fat

Calories	161
Calories from Fat	75
Total Fat	8 g
Saturated Fat	3 g
Cholesterol	96 mg
Sodium	428 mg
Total Carbohydrate	9 g
Dietary Fiber	1 g
Sugars	5 g
Protein	13 g

1 Preheat the oven to 350 degrees. In a 10- to 11-inch deep-sided nonstick skillet with oven-proof handle (or similar stove-top and oven-proof casserole) over medium heat, combine the oil, onion, and mushrooms. Cook the vegetables, stirring frequently, until the onion is limp and just beginning to brown, about 4 minutes.

2 Sprinkle the croutons, then the salt, over the vegetable mixture. Cook, stirring, until the croutons are heated through, about 1 1/2 minutes longer.

3 Remove the skillet from the heat. Evenly spread out the vegetable-crouton mixture in the skillet (or transfer it to a lightly greased 10-inch pie plate). Sprinkle the roasted peppers over top.

4 In a medium bowl, beat together the eggs, egg substitute, milk, half the cheese, the mustard, and pepper with a fork until well blended. Pour the mixture over the vegetables. Sprinkle the remaining cheese evenly over top.

5 Turn down the oven to 325 degrees. Transfer the skillet to the oven and bake on the center oven rack for 17 to 22 minutes, or until the frittata is barely set in the center when the dish is jiggled.

6 Transfer to a cooling rack; let stand for 5 minutes. Cut into wedges and serve using a wide-bladed spatula.

MEDITERRANEAN SPINACH BAKE

This vegetarian dish makes a tasty luncheon or dinner entree. The number of bread slices needed will depend on their size.

3 to 4 slices multi-grain or whole-wheat bread

1 1/2 Tbsp olive oil

1/2 cup chopped onion

2 cups frozen loose-leaf spinach

1 1/2 tsp dried dill weed

Scant 1/4 tsp salt (optional)

1/8 tsp black pepper

1/2 cup crumbled low-fat feta cheese

1 cup fat-free ricotta cheese

1/2 cup shredded fat-free mozzarella cheese

1 cup liquid egg substitute

PREP TIME: 15 MINUTES

SERVINGS: 6

SERVING SIZE: 1/6 OF BAKE

Exchanges
1/2 Starch
1 Vegetable
1/2 Skim Milk
1 High-Fat Meat

Calories 207
   Calories from Fat 63
Total Fat . . . . .7 g
   Saturated Fat . . . . .2 g
Cholesterol . . . . .12 mg
Sodium . . . . .466 mg
Total Carbohydrate . . . .18 g
   Dietary Fiber . . . . .4 g
   Sugars . . . . .4 g
Protein . . . . .18 g

1 Spray a 9-inch square baking pan with nonstick spray. Arrange 1 layer of bread slices in the bottom of the pan, cutting to fit, if necessary. Set aside. Preheat the oven to 375 degrees.

2 In a nonstick skillet over medium heat, combine the oil and onion. Cook the onion, stirring frequently, until it is soft but not browned. Stir in the spinach. Cover, reduce heat, and cook gently for 4 to 5 minutes, stirring occasionally and breaking up any large lumps of spinach if necessary.

3 Meanwhile, in a medium-sized bowl, stir together the seasonings, cheeses, and egg substitute.

4 Remove the pan from the burner. Stir the spinach mixture into the cheese mixture. Cover the bread slices with the mixture, spreading evenly with the back of a large spoon.

5 Bake for about 30 to 35 minutes or until the filling is cooked through.

VEGETARIAN LASAGNA

Here's a tasty vegetarian lasagna, made with convenient, oven-ready (no-boiling required) noodles; they are usually stocked with the regular lasagna pasta. Since the noodles are shorter than conventional ones, lay them crosswise rather than lengthwise in the pan.

1 Tbsp olive oil

1 large onion, chopped

2 medium celery stalks, chopped

1 medium zucchini, chopped

1 1/2 cups chopped mushrooms

1 tsp dried thyme leaves

1 26-oz jar spicy red pepper or herbed tomato pasta sauce or spaghetti sauce

1 15-oz can no-salt-added tomato sauce

1/4 tsp ground black pepper

1/4 tsp salt (optional)

2 1/4 cups 1 percent fat cottage cheese (not salt-free), preferably small curd

9 no-boil (oven-ready) lasagna noodles

1 8-oz package shredded fat-free mozzarella cheese, divided

2 Tbsp grated Parmesan cheese

PREP TIME: 25 MINUTES

SERVINGS: 9

SERVING SIZE: 1/9 LASAGNA

Exchanges
2 Starch
2 Vegetable
2 Lean Meat

Calories 297
  Calories from Fat 45
Total Fat . . . . .5 g
  Saturated Fat . . . . . . .1 g
Cholesterol . . . . .8 mg
Sodium . . . . .700 mg
Total Carbohydrate . . . .40 g
  Dietary Fiber . . . . .4 g
  Sugars . . . . .9 g
Protein . . . . .23 g

1 Preheat the oven to 350 degrees.

2 In a large pot over medium-high heat, combine the oil, onion, celery, zucchini, mushrooms, and thyme. Cook, stirring, until the vegetables are softened and excess liquid is reduced, 6 to 8 minutes.

3 Add the pasta sauce, tomato sauce, and pepper. Bring to a boil. Reduce the heat and simmer, stirring occasionally, 5 minutes longer to blend flavors. Taste and add salt, if desired.

4 If a smoother consistency is desired for cottage cheese layers, process briefly in a food processor (optional).

5 Spread 1 1/4 cups sauce in the bottom of a greased 9 1/2- × 13-inch pan. Arrange a layer of 3 noodles over the sauce. Top with 1/2 the cottage cheese, spreading it out evenly. Sprinkle with 1/2 the mozzarella cheese. Add 1/3 of the remaining sauce.

6 Add another layer of 3 noodles, then the remaining cottage cheese, then the remaining mozzarella. Add scant 1/3 of the remaining sauce. Add the final layer of noodles. Cover evenly with the remaining sauce. Sprinkle with the Parmesan cheese.

7 Cover with aluminum foil and bake in the middle third of the oven for 35 minutes. Uncover and bake 5 to 10 minutes longer, until the pasta in the center is cooked through when tested with a fork. Let the lasagna stand for 5 minutes before cutting into 9 portions.

CHICKEN KABOB DINNER

"Chicken makes a great kabob. We like to make this dinner with small white onions. If they are unavailable, substitute medium onions and quarter them."

MARINADE

    3 *Tbsp olive oil*

    3 *Tbsp fat-free low-sodium or regular chicken broth*

    1/4 *cup fresh lemon juice*

    1/2 *cup chopped onion*

    1/4 *cup coarsely chopped fresh parsley leaves*

    1 *tsp minced garlic*

    1/2 *tsp dried marjoram leaves*

1 1/2 *tsp dried thyme leaves*

    1/4 *tsp salt (optional)*

CHICKEN, VEGETABLES, AND RICE

    1 *lb boneless, skinless chicken breast, cut into 1 1/4-inch pieces*

    8 *small white onions*

    1 *green bell pepper, trimmed, seeded, and cut into 2-inch pieces*

    1 *small zucchini, cut into 1/2 inch-thick rounds*

    1 *cup uncooked basmati rice, cooked according to package directions*

PREP TIME: 25 MINUTES

SERVINGS: 4

SERVING SIZE: 4 OZ MEAT, PLUS VEGETABLES AND 3/4 CUP RICE

Exchanges
2 1/2 Starch
2 Vegetable
2 Lean Meat
1/2 Fat

Calories 409
  Calories from Fat 85
Total Fat . . . . .9 g
  Saturated Fat . . . . .2 g
Cholesterol . . . . .68 mg
Sodium . . . . .82 mg
Total Carbohydrate . . . .50 g
  Dietary Fiber . . . . .4 g
  Sugars . . . . .6 g
Protein . . . . .31 g

1 To make the marinade: In a medium non-reactive bowl, combine the oil, broth, lemon juice, chopped onion, parsley, garlic, marjoram leaves, thyme leaves, and salt. Stir to mix well. Add the chicken, and stir until well coated. Cover and refrigerate 1 hour, stirring occasionally.

2 Meanwhile, place the white onions in a large saucepan of boiling water. Parboil over medium heat for 3 or 4 minutes. Add the pepper pieces, and boil an additional 2 minutes. Drain in a colander. Trim and peel the onions.

3 Remove the chicken pieces as needed from the marinade with a slotted spoon. Alternate green peppers, onions, and zucchini with chicken pieces on 2 or 3 large skewers. Pack the skewers tightly, as this will help keep the vegetables from shifting as the skewers are turned during grilling.

4 To grill, place the chicken and vegetable skewers on a charcoal or gas grill, and cook 12 to 15 minutes depending on the heat and the degree of doneness desired. Turn frequently so that the meat and vegetables can cook evenly.

5 To broil, rest the ends of the skewers on the rim of a baking pan so that the fat from the meat can drip into the pan during broiling. Broil about 5 inches from the heat for 12 to 15 minutes, depending on the degree of doneness desired; turn frequently so that the meat and vegetables can cook evenly.

6 Put rice on a serving platter and arrange kabobs on top. Use a fork to slide the meat and vegetables off the skewers onto the platter.

BEEF KABOB DINNER

Cook these colorful beef kabobs on the grill or in the broiler.

1/4 cup fat-free low-sodium or
    regular chicken broth

1/4 cup lite soy sauce

  1 tsp sugar

1/2 tsp ground ginger

  1 Tbsp sesame seeds

  1 Tbsp Asian sesame oil

1/4 tsp hot pepper sauce

  1 lb sirloin steak, trimmed of all fat and
    cut into 1 1/2-inch pieces

12 pearl onions

  1 sweet red or green bell pepper, seeded
    and cut into 12 pieces

12 cherry tomatoes, stems removed

  1 cup brown or long-grain white rice,
    cooked according to package directions

PREP TIME: 25 MINUTES

SERVINGS: 4

SERVING SIZE: 4 OZ MEAT,
  3 EACH PEPPER PIECES,
  ONIONS, AND TOMATOES,
  PLUS 3/4 CUP RICE

Exchanges
2 1/2 Starch
2 Vegetable
2 Lean Meat
1/2 Fat

Calories 390
  Calories from Fat 86
Total Fat . . . . .10 g
  Saturated Fat . . . . .3 g
Cholesterol . . . . .64 mg
Sodium . . . . .536 mg
Total Carbohydrate . . . .48 g
  Dietary Fiber . . . . .4 g
  Sugars . . . . .8 g
Protein . . . . .28 g

1 In a medium non-reactive bowl, combine the broth, soy sauce, sugar, ginger, sesame seeds, oil, and pepper sauce. Stir to mix well. Add the beef cubes. Stir to mix well.

2 Cover and refrigerate about 6 hours, stirring occasionally.

3 In a large pot, add the onions to boiling water, and cook 2 to 3 minutes. Add the pepper pieces, and cook an additional 1 or 2 minutes. Drain in a colander. Trim and peel the onions.

4 Remove the beef pieces as needed from the marinade with a slotted spoon. Alternate peppers and onions with the beef on 2 or 3 large skewers. Pack the skewers tightly, as this will help keep the vegetables from shifting as the skewers are turned during grilling. Thread the tomatoes on a separate skewer, and set aside.

5 To grill, place the meat and vegetable skewers on a charcoal or gas grill, and cook 20 to 30 minutes depending on the heat and the degree of doneness desired; turn often for even cooking.

6 To broil, rest the ends of the skewers on the rim of a baking pan so that the fat from the meat can drip into the pan during broiling. Broil about 5 inches from the heat for 25 to 30 minutes, depending on the degree of doneness desired; turn frequently so that the meat and vegetables can cook evenly.

7 During the last 5 minutes of cooking, broil or grill the tomatoes, turning frequently.

8 To serve, arrange the rice on a large serving platter. Place kabobs on the rice. Use a fork to slide the meat and vegetables off the skewers onto the rice.

SKILLET DINNERS

CHICKEN-ASPARAGUS STIR-FRY WITH SESAME

"Both the nutty taste of toasted oriental sesame oil and sesame seeds help bring out the flavor in this savory chicken-asparagus dish. The crisp-tender asparagus and crunchy sesame seeds also add pleasing texture."

1 lb boneless, skinless chicken breast, cut into 1-inch cubes

3 Tbsp lite soy sauce, divided

2 Tbsp Asian sesame oil, divided

1 clove garlic, peeled and minced

1 1/2 lb fresh asparagus

2 Tbsp sesame seeds

1/3 cup fat-free low-sodium or regular chicken broth

2 tsp cornstarch

2 cups hot cooked brown or white rice

PREP TIME: 20 MINUTES

SERVINGS: 4

SERVING SIZE: 1 CUP, PLUS 1/2 CUP COOKED RICE

Exchanges
1 1/2 Starch
1 Vegetable
3 Very Lean Meat
2 Fat

Calories	.359
Calories from Fat	.117
Total Fat	.13 g
Saturated Fat	.3 g
Cholesterol	.68 mg
Sodium	.569 mg
Total Carbohydrate	.29 g
Dietary Fiber	.4 g
Sugars	.4 g
Protein	.31 g

1 Combine the chicken, 1 1/2 tablespoons soy sauce, 1 tablespoon sesame oil, and garlic in a medium bowl, stirring to mix. Let stand while the remaining ingredients are prepared.

2 Break off the tough ends (3 to 4 inches) of the asparagus spears and discard. Cut the spears on a diagonal into 1 1/4-inch pieces.

3 In a 12-inch stir-fry pan or deep-sided nonstick skillet over medium-high heat, toast the sesame seeds, stirring, until they turn light brown. Immediately turn out the seeds onto a paper towel.

4 In a medium bowl, stir together the chicken broth, cornstarch, and remaining 1 1/2 tablespoons soy sauce until blended.

5 In the stir-fry pan previously used, combine the reserved 1 tablespoon oil and the asparagus. Cook over medium-high heat, stirring frequently, 3 or 4 minutes or until the pieces are almost tender when tested with a fork. Turn out the asparagus into the bowl containing the chicken broth mixture.

6 Raise heat to high and add the chicken pieces and any unabsorbed seasoning to the skillet. Cook, stirring constantly, 3 or 4 minutes or until the chicken pieces are lightly browned and just cooked through.

7 Return the reserved asparagus and broth mixture to the skillet. Continue cooking, stirring, until the asparagus is piping hot and the pan liquid is just slightly thickened.

8 Sprinkle the dish with the toasted sesame seeds. Serve over hot cooked rice.

Chicken and Vegetables in Spicy Peanut Sauce

This dish is savory, colorful, and easy to prepare. You can adjust the spiciness to your taste by choosing a mild to hot picante sauce and curry powder.

1 lb boneless, skinless chicken breast, cut into 3/4-inch cubes

1/4 cup mild to hot picante sauce or salsa

1 Tbsp mild to hot curry powder

1 Tbsp peanut oil or corn oil

1 medium onion, chopped

3 cups small broccoli florets

1 cup cubed (1/2-inch) red bell pepper

1 8-oz can low-sodium or regular tomato sauce

1 4-oz can chopped mild green chiles, drained

3 Tbsp smooth peanut butter

2 Tbsp lite soy sauce

Salt and black pepper to taste (optional)

2 cups hot cooked brown or white rice

PREP TIME: 25 MINUTES

SERVINGS: 5

SERVING SIZE: 1 CUP CHICKEN MIXTURE WITH SAUCE, PLUS 1/2 CUP RICE

Exchanges
1 1/2 Starch
2 Vegetable
3 Very Lean Meat
1 1/2 Fat

Calories	331
Calories from Fat	100
Total Fat	11 g
Saturated Fat	2 g
Cholesterol	55 mg
Sodium	572 mg
Total Carbohydrate	31 g
Dietary Fiber	6 g
Sugars	9 g
Protein	27 g

1 Stir together the chicken, picante sauce, and curry powder in a medium bowl. Let stand while remaining ingredients are readied.

2 In a 12-inch nonstick skillet over medium-high heat, heat oil to hot but not smoking. Add the chicken pieces and the onion to the skillet. Cook over medium-high heat, stirring, 4 or 5 minutes or until the chicken pieces are just cooked through. Turn out the chicken and onion into a bowl and reserve.

3 Add the broccoli, bell pepper, and 1/4 cup water to the skillet. Cook, stirring frequently, 3 or 4 minutes until the vegetables are almost cooked through.

4 In a small, deep bowl, stir together the tomato sauce, green chiles, peanut butter, and soy sauce until the sauce is very well blended.

5 Return the chicken mixture to the skillet. Stir in the peanut sauce. Place over medium-high heat and cook until piping hot. Add salt and pepper to taste, if desired. Thin the sauce with a tablespoon or two of water, if necessary.

6 Serve the chicken-vegetable mixture and sauce spooned over the rice.

GREEK-STYLE CHICKEN

This easy chicken dish combines some classic flavors from Greek cuisine. Cutting the chicken into bite-sized pieces shortens the cooking time considerably.

1 *Tbsp olive oil*

3/4 *lb boneless, skinless chicken breast, cut into bite-sized pieces*

1 *green bell pepper, seeded and chopped*

1 *tsp minced garlic*

1 *15-oz can low-sodium or regular tomato sauce*

1/3 *cup fat-free low-sodium or regular chicken broth*

1/4 *cup Kalamata black olives, drained, pitted, and chopped*

1 *tsp dried thyme leaves*

1/4 *cup crumbled feta cheese*

1 *cup brown or white rice, cooked according to package directions*

PREP TIME: 18 MINUTES

SERVINGS: 4

SERVING SIZE: 3/4 CUP, PLUS 3/4 CUP RICE

Exchanges
2 1/2 Starch
1 Vegetable
2 Lean Meat
1/2 Fat

Calories 371
  Calories from Fat 81
Total Fat . . . . .9 g
  Saturated Fat . . . . . . .3 g
Cholesterol . . . . .58 mg
Sodium . . . . .275 mg
Total Carbohydrate . . . .46 g
  Dietary Fiber . . . . . . .4 g
  Sugars . . . . .8 g
Protein . . . . .25 g

1 In a large skillet, combine the oil, chicken, green pepper, and garlic. Cook over medium heat, stirring frequently, until the chicken is white on all sides, about 8 minutes.

2 Add the tomato sauce, broth, olives, and thyme. Bring to a boil; reduce the heat, cover, and simmer, stirring occasionally, about 10 minutes until the chicken is almost tender.

3 Stir in the feta cheese. Uncover, raise heat, and cook an additional 5 minutes, until flavors have blended and sauce has thickened slightly. Serve over rice.

Kung Pao Chicken

> Here's a healthy variation of a classic Chinese recipe that you can easily make at home. The crunchy peanuts make a wonderful contrast to the chicken.

MARINADE

> 1 1/2 Tbsp lite soy sauce
>
> 2 tsp rice or white wine vinegar
>
> 6 to 10 drops hot pepper sauce, or to taste (optional)
>
> 1 Tbsp finely chopped fresh ginger, or 1 tsp ground ginger
>
> 1 green onion, sliced

CHICKEN, VEGETABLES, AND PEANUTS

> 3/4 lb boneless, skinless chicken breast, cut into bite-sized pieces
>
> 1 cup thinly sliced cabbage
>
> 1 celery stalk, sliced
>
> 2 oz (1/4 cup) dry-roasted salted peanuts
>
> 1 Tbsp canola oil
>
> 2 Tbsp fat-free reduced-sodium chicken broth

SEASONINGS AND RICE

> 1 Tbsp lite soy sauce
>
> 1 Tbsp Splenda
>
> 1 tsp rice or white wine vinegar
>
> 1 cup uncooked white rice, cooked according to package directions, but prepared without fat or salt

PREP TIME: 30 MINUTES

SERVINGS: 4

SERVING SIZE: 1 CUP MEAT MIXTURE, PLUS 1/2 CUP RICE

Exchanges
1 Starch
2 Vegetable
3 Lean Meat
1/2 Fat

Calories 320
  Calories from Fat . . .108
Total Fat . . . . .12 g
  Saturated Fat . . . . . . .2 g
Cholesterol . . . . .49 mg
Sodium . . . . .519 mg
Total Carbohydrate . . . .27 g
  Dietary Fiber . . . . .3 g
  Sugars . . . . .3 g
Protein . . . . .26 g

1 In a large, non-reactive bowl, mix soy sauce, vinegar, hot pepper sauce, ginger, and onions. Stir in the chicken. Cover and marinate 15 minutes at room temperature (or up to 12 hours if refrigerated).

2 In a large skillet over medium-high heat, cook the cabbage, celery, and peanuts in the oil and broth until the vegetables are crisp-tender, stirring, about 3 or 4 minutes. With a slotted spoon, transfer the vegetables and nuts to a bowl.

3 Add the marinated chicken and marinade to the skillet. Cook the chicken over medium heat, stirring, until it changes color, about 3 minutes. Add the soy sauce, Splenda, and vinegar, along with the reserved peanuts and vegetables. Cook, stirring, an additional 3 or 4 minutes until the chicken is cooked through. Serve over white rice.

SZECHUAN-STYLE CHICKEN AND GREEN BEANS

"You don't have to go to a restaurant to get a great Chinese meal. Here's a dish we enjoy at home on a regular basis."

MARINADE

    2 Tbsp lite soy sauce

    2 Tbsp water

    1 1/2 Tbsp Asian sesame oil

    2 tsp rice or white wine vinegar

    1 1/2 tsp granulated sugar

    1/2 tsp ground ginger

    3 to 4 drops hot pepper sauce (optional)

CHICKEN, BEANS, AND RICE

    1 lb boneless, skinless chicken breast, cut into bite-sized pieces

    3 1/2 cups petite frozen green bean pieces

    1/4 cup thinly sliced green onion tops

    1 1/4 cups uncooked long-grain white rice, cooked according to package directions

PREP TIME: 25 MINUTES

SERVINGS: 5

SERVING SIZE: 1 CUP, PLUS 3/4 CUP RICE

Exchanges
2 1/2 Starch
1 Vegetable
2 Very Lean Meat
1 Fat

Calories 348
  Calories from Fat 61
Total Fat . . . . .7 g
  Saturated Fat . . . . .2 g
Cholesterol . . . . .55 mg
Sodium . . . . .302 mg
Total Carbohydrate . . . .45 g
  Dietary Fiber . . . . .4 g
  Sugars . . . . .5 g
Protein . . . . .25 g

1 In a medium bowl, combine the soy sauce, water, oil, vinegar, sugar, ginger, and hot pepper sauce, if desired. Stir to mix well. Add the chicken, and stir to coat. Marinate 10 minutes.

2 Meanwhile, cook the beans according to package directions. Drain in a colander, and reserve.

3 Remove the chicken from the marinade with a slotted spoon, and transfer to a large, nonstick skillet. Cook over medium heat, stirring frequently until the chicken turns white on all sides, about 4 or 5 minutes.

4 Add the remaining marinade, and stir to mix. Bring to a boil. Reduce the heat to medium, cover, and simmer an additional 5 or 6 minutes, stirring occasionally, until the chicken is partially cooked. Stir in the green beans and cook, uncovered, an additional 2 minutes. Stir in the green onions and cook, uncovered, an additional 1 or 2 minutes. Serve over rice.

Sesame-Noodle Stir-Fry with Chicken

Toasting sesame seeds heightens their flavor and crunchiness, so they add great appeal in this Singapore-style dish. This recipe calls for broccoli slaw, a ready-to-use slaw mix that is often sold in supermarkets with other bags of ready-to-use greens. Though shredded nearly as fine as cabbage slaw, the broccoli version (made from peeled, tender broccoli stems and some shredded carrot) holds its shape during stir-frying.

1 lb boneless, skinless chicken breast, cut into 2- x 1/8-inch strips

3 Tbsp lite soy sauce, divided

2 to 3 tsp mild or medium hot curry powder, divided

Pinch hot red pepper flakes (optional)

2 Tbsp sesame seeds

3 Tbsp peanut oil or corn oil, divided

2 cups broccoli slaw mix

3 1/2 cups coarsely sliced green cabbage

5 or 6 green onions (including tender tops), cut crosswise into 1 1/2-inch pieces

2 cups cooked Chinese lo mein noodles or cooked vermicelli (thin spaghetti), cut into 3-inch lengths

Prep Time: 20 minutes

Servings: 7

Serving Size: 1 cup

Exchanges
1 Starch
1 Vegetable
2 Very Lean Meat
1 Fat

Calories	218
Calories from Fat	81
Total Fat	9 g
Saturated Fat	2 g
Cholesterol	39 mg
Sodium	309 mg
Total Carbohydrate	17 g
Dietary Fiber	3 g
Sugars	3 g
Protein	18 g

1 In a medium bowl stir together the chicken, 1 1/2 tablespoons soy sauce, 1 teaspoon curry powder, and hot red pepper flakes (if desired). Set aside while the remaining ingredients are readied.

2 In a 12-inch nonstick stir-fry pan or deep-sided skillet, heat the sesame seeds over medium-high heat. Toast the seeds, stirring, until they begin to brown and become fragrant, about 2 minutes. Immediately turn out the seeds into a large bowl.

3 In the pan used for the seeds, heat half the peanut oil over high heat until hot but not smoking. Add the broccoli slaw; cook, stirring, for 1 1/2 minutes. Add the cabbage and green onions and continue to cook, stirring, 1 to 2 minutes or until the broccoli is almost cooked through. Turn out the slaw mixture into the bowl with the sesame seeds, stirring to blend.

4 Add the remaining peanut oil to the pan; heat to hot but not smoking. Add the chicken to the pan. Cook, stirring, about 3 to 4 minutes longer until the chicken pieces are just cooked through.

5 Stir in the reserved vegetable-sesame seed mixture and cooked noodles. Stir in the remaining 1 1/2 tablespoons soy sauce and 1 teaspoon curry powder. Cook, stirring, until the ingredients are well combined and just heated through. Taste and add more curry powder, if desired.

Handy Tip

If you can't find broccoli slaw, you can substitute 1 1/2 cups finely chopped broccoli florets and 1/2 cup shredded carrots. The texture and appearance of the dish will be a little different, but it will still be good.

LEMON-TARRAGON CHICKEN WITH VEGETABLE PILAF

"This is an easy skillet featuring tender, tarragon-flecked chicken breast pieces cooked and served with a colorful and savory vegetable-rice pilaf."

2 Tbsp fresh lemon juice

1 Tbsp plus 1 tsp Dijon or Dijon-style mustard

2 tsp dried tarragon leaves

2 tsp clover honey or other mild-flavored honey

4 4-oz boneless skinless chicken breast halves, halved lengthwise

1 1/2 Tbsp olive oil

1 large onion, chopped

2 medium celery stalks, chopped

3 medium carrots, diced

2/3 cup fat-free low-sodium or regular chicken broth

1/4 cup quick-cooking rice

Salt and black pepper to taste (optional)

PREP TIME: 25 MINUTES

SERVINGS: 4

SERVING SIZE: 1 4-OZ CHICKEN BREAST HALF, PLUS 2/3 CUP VEGETABLE PILAF

Exchanges
1 Starch
1 Vegetable
3 Very Lean Meat
1 1/2 Fat

Calories 269
　Calories from Fat 71
Total Fat . . . . .8 g
　Saturated Fat . . . . .2 g
Cholesterol . . . . .68 mg
Sodium . . . . .312 mg
Total Carbohydrate . . . .21 g
　Dietary Fiber . . . . .3 g
　Sugars . . . . .11 g
Protein . . . . .28 g

1 Stir together the lemon juice, mustard, tarragon, and honey in a medium, non-reactive bowl. Add the chicken, turning till coated. Let stand while the remaining ingredients are readied.

2 In a 12-inch or similar nonstick skillet over medium-high heat, combine the oil, onion, celery, and carrots. Cook, stirring, until the onion is limp, about 4 minutes.

3 Add the chicken pieces to the skillet; reserve any lemon marinade in the bowl. Cook the chicken pieces over medium-high heat, turning frequently, about 7 minutes or until the pieces are browned all over.

4 Add 1/4 cup chicken broth to the skillet. Bring to a simmer and cook, stirring frequently until the chicken is almost cooked through, about 8 or 9 minutes longer. If necessary, occasionally add a few teaspoons broth to keep the pan from boiling dry.

5 Push the chicken pieces to one side. Stir in the reserved marinade, another 1/3 cup chicken broth, and the rice. Cover and simmer about 4 minutes longer, or until the rice is just tender. Add salt and black pepper to taste.

Singapore Chicken

Curry and soy sauce make a great flavor combination for this easy chicken skillet dish. It is served over rice, so if you're in a hurry use quick-cooking or perhaps leftover rice. Since brown rice is better nutritionally than white, but takes longer to cook, consider readying a batch ahead and stashing it in the freezer to thaw and use as needed, or buy ready-to-use cartons at the supermarket.

1 medium onion, chopped

1 Tbsp peanut or canola oil

1 cup fat-free reduced-sodium or regular chicken broth, divided

1 lb boneless, skinless chicken breast meat, cut into bite-sized pieces

1 to 2 1/2 tsp mild curry powder, or to taste

1/8 tsp black pepper (optional)

3 Tbsp unsalted or salted peanuts, coarsely chopped

2 Tbsp lite soy sauce

1 Tbsp cornstarch

1 1/2 cups small cauliflower or broccoli florets (or a combination)

1/2 cup coarsely diced red bell pepper

1/4 tsp salt to taste (optional)

2 cups cooked brown or white rice

PREP TIME: 20 MINUTES

SERVINGS: 4

SERVING SIZE: 1 CUP CHICKEN AND VEGETABLES, PLUS 1/2 CUP RICE

Exchanges
2 Starch
1 Vegetable
3 Very Lean Meat
1 Fat

Calories 345
   Calories from Fat 81
Total Fat . . . . .9 g
   Saturated Fat . . . . .2 g
Cholesterol . . . . .66 mg
Sodium . . . . .475 mg
Total Carbohydrate . . . .33 g
   Dietary Fiber . . . . .5 g
   Sugars . . . . .7 g
Protein . . . . .33 g

1 In a 12-inch nonstick skillet, combine the onion, oil, and 1 tablespoon of the chicken broth. Cook over medium heat, stirring frequently, until the onion is tender, about 5 or 6 minutes.

2 Push the onion to the side of the pan. Add the chicken. Sprinkle on the curry powder and black pepper, if desired. Add the chopped peanuts. Cook over medium heat, stirring frequently, until the chicken is opaque, about 4 minutes. If the chicken begins to stick or burn, add a little more of the chicken broth.

3 Stir together the soy sauce and cornstarch until well blended. Thoroughly stir the remaining chicken broth and the soy sauce mixture into the pan until blended. Add the cauliflower (and/or broccoli) and bell pepper to the skillet, stirring well. Cook over medium heat, stirring, until the chicken is cooked through, about 3 to 4 minutes. Add salt to taste, if desired.

4 Serve the chicken and vegetables over rice.

CHICKEN, EGGPLANT, AND BELL PEPPER SKILLET

Along with soy sauce, chili paste with garlic is the key seasoning in this flavorful, slightly spicy dish. Since some brands of chili paste (also known as chili puree with garlic) are spicier than others, start with 1 tablespoon and add more at the end of cooking, if desired. Chili paste with garlic is stocked with the Asian or Chinese seasonings in many supermarkets. This recipe calls for ready-to-use chicken breast cubes, a handy short-cut ingredient when you're in a hurry. Chopped onions from a salad bar are also a time-saver.

1 lb chicken breast cubes (about 1-inch cubes)

1/2 cup chopped salad bar onions or green onions (or 1 small onion, chopped)

3 Tbsp lite soy sauce, divided

1 to 1 1/2 Tbsp chili paste (or puree) with garlic, to taste

2 1/2 Tbsp peanut oil or canola oil, divided

1 1-lb eggplant, peeled and cut into generous 1-inch chunks

1 medium red or green bell pepper, cut into 1-inch chunks

1 Tbsp cornstarch combined with 1/3 cup cold water

2 cups hot cooked brown or white rice

PREP TIME: 20 MINUTES

SERVINGS: 5

SERVING SIZE: 1 CUP CHICKEN AND VEGETABLES, PLUS 1/2 CUP RICE

Exchanges
1 1/2 Starch
3 Vegetable
1/2 Fat
1 Lean Meat

Calories 269
   Calories from Fat 60
Total Fat . . . . .7 g
   Saturated Fat . . . . .2 g
Cholesterol . . . . .20 mg
Sodium . . . . .1383 mg
Total Carbohydrate . . . .36 g

1 Stir together the chicken, onion, 1 tablespoon soy sauce, and 1 tablespoon hot chili paste in a medium bowl. Let stand while the remaining ingredients are readied.

2 In a 12-inch or larger nonstick stir-fry pan or deep-sided 12-inch nonstick skillet over medium-high heat, heat 1 1/2 tablespoons oil to hot but not smoking. Add the eggplant, the remaining 2 tablespoons soy sauce, and 2 tablespoons water. Cook the eggplant, stirring, for 3 minutes. Add a little more water if the pan begins to boil dry.

3 Add the bell pepper to the pan. Continue cooking, stirring, until the eggplant is almost tender when pierced with a fork, about 1 minute longer. Turn out the vegetables into a medium bowl and reserve.

4 Add the remaining 1 tablespoon oil to the pan and heat to hot but not smoking. Add the chicken mixture. Cook, stirring, adjusting the heat so the chicken cooks briskly but does not burn, until the pieces are just cooked through, 4 to 5 minutes.

5 Return the vegetables to the stir-fry pan. Stir in the cornstarch-water mixture and continue cooking, stirring, just until the chicken is cooked through and the vegetables are piping hot. Taste and stir in 1/2 tablespoon more chili paste with garlic, if desired. Serve over rice.

ASIAN-STYLE TURKEY CUTLET SKILLET

"Here's a simple way to lend an Asian twist to a package of those very healthful and convenient turkey breast cutlets."

3 Tbsp lite soy sauce, divided

3 Tbsp chopped fresh cilantro leaves

3 or 4 green onions, including tender tops, cut into 1/2-inch pieces

1 1/2 Tbsp peanut oil or corn oil, divided

4 4-oz turkey breast cutlets

2 medium celery stalks, cut on a diagonal into thin slices

1 large carrot, peeled and cut on a diagonal into thin slices

1 cup coarsely sliced mushrooms

3 to 6 Tbsp fat-free low-sodium or regular chicken broth

Salt and black pepper to taste (optional)

PREP TIME: 25 MINUTES

SERVINGS: 4

SERVING SIZE: 1 4-OZ CUTLET, PLUS SCANT 1/2 CUP VEGETABLES

Exchanges
4 Very Lean Meat
1 Vegetable
1 Fat

Calories 195
    Calories from Fat 53
Total Fat . . . . .6 g
    Saturated Fat . . . . .1 g
Cholesterol . . . . .73 mg
Sodium . . . . .572 mg
Total Carbohydrate . . . . .6 g
    Dietary Fiber . . . . .2 g
    Sugars . . . . .3 g
Protein . . . . .28 g

1 In a flat glass dish large enough to hold the cutlets, combine 2 tablespoons soy sauce, cilantro, green onion, and 1/2 tablespoon oil. Dip the cutlets into the mixture on one side and then the other until coated. Let stand in the dish while the remaining ingredients are readied.

2 In a 12-inch nonstick skillet, heat the remaining 1 tablespoon oil over high heat until hot but not smoking. Add the celery, carrots, and mushrooms. Cook briskly, stirring frequently, until the vegetables are limp, about 3 minutes. If the skillet begins to burn or boil dry, add a little broth as needed.

3 Push the vegetables to one side. Add 3 tablespoons broth and remaining tablespoon of soy sauce to the skillet. Add the turkey cutlets and optional salt and black pepper to taste, if desired (and any leftover seasonings in bowl). Reduce the heat slightly. Turning the cutlets occasionally, cook until they are well browned all over and cooked through when cut into in the thickest part, 7 to 12 minutes longer. Add a little more broth if necessary to keep the skillet from boiling dry.

Hamburger Stroganoff

If you've never tried nonfat sour cream, you'll be surprised at the rich, creamy texture it can give to a sauce. Some brands taste better than others, so experiment to find out which you like best. We like hamburger stroganoff better than beef stroganoff because the ground meat absorbs the flavor of the sauce so well.

1 lb ground beef round

1 medium onion, finely chopped

1/2 lb fresh mushrooms, washed, trimmed, and sliced

1 tsp minced garlic

1 cup fat-free beef broth

2 Tbsp tomato paste

2 tsp Dijon-style mustard

1 tsp dried thyme leaves

1 large bay leaf

1/4 tsp black pepper

1/4 tsp salt, or to taste (optional)

1 cup nonfat sour cream

4 oz (1 generous cup) uncooked eggless egg noodles, cooked according to package directions

Parsley sprigs for garnish (optional)

PREP TIME: 10 MINUTES

SERVINGS: 4

SERVING SIZE: 1 CUP, PLUS 1 OZ EGG NOODLES

Exchanges
2 1/2 Carbohydrate
3 Lean Meat

Calories 327
    Calories from Fat 81
Total Fat . . . . .9 g
    Saturated Fat . . . . .1 g
Cholesterol . . . . .62 mg
Sodium . . . . .456 mg
Total Carbohydrate . . . .38 g
    Dietary Fiber . . . . .3 g
    Sugars . . . . .9 g
Protein . . . . .32 g

1 In a large nonstick skillet, brown the meat, onion, mushrooms, and garlic over medium-high heat, stirring frequently, about 6 or 7 minutes or until the meat is browned and the onion is tender.

2 Stir together the broth, tomato paste, and mustard. Stir into the meat mixture.

3 Add the thyme, bay leaf, pepper, and salt, if desired, and stir to mix well. Cover and simmer 15 minutes, stirring occasionally, or until flavors are well blended.

4 Reduce the heat under the skillet so that the liquid does not boil. Stir the sour cream into the broth. Heat 2 or 3 minutes longer.

5 Serve individual portions of the stroganoff over noodles. Garnish with parsley sprigs, if desired.

BEEF AND ARTICHOKE SKILLET

"Beef and artichokes make an unusual combination with an Italian accent."

1 lb thin-cut round steak, trimmed
of all fat and cut into small strips

Salt (optional) and pepper to taste

1 cup chopped onion

1 large red bell pepper, seeded and cut
into 1/2 inch–wide strips

1 Tbsp olive oil

1/2 cup fat-free low-sodium or regular
chicken broth, divided

1 15-oz can low-sodium or regular tomato
sauce

1 13 3/4-oz can water-packed artichoke
heart quarters, drained and tough outer
leaves discarded

1 1/2 tsp Italian seasoning

4 oz (about 1 1/4 cups) penne pasta,
cooked according to package
directions

PREP TIME: 20 MINUTES

SERVINGS: 5

SERVING SIZE: 1 CUP

Exchanges
1 Starch
2 Vegetable
2 Lean Meat
1/2 Fat

Calories 272
   Calories from Fat 64
Total Fat . . . . .7 g
   Saturated Fat . . . . .2 g
Cholesterol . . . . .47 mg
Sodium . . . . .242 mg
Total Carbohydrate . . . .30 g
   Dietary Fiber . . . . .4 g
   Sugars . . . . .9 g
Protein . . . . .21 g

1 Sprinkle the round steak with salt, if desired, and pepper. In a 12-inch nonstick skillet coated with nonstick spray, cook the round steak over medium heat until browned on all sides, stirring frequently, about 4 to 5 minutes. Remove with a slotted spoon, and reserve.

2 In the skillet, combine the onion, pepper, oil, and 2 tablespoons of the broth. Cook over medium heat, stirring frequently, until the onion is tender, about 5 to 6 minutes.

3 Return the meat to the pan. Add the tomato sauce and remaining broth. Add the artichoke hearts and Italian seasoning. Stir to mix well. Bring to a boil. Reduce the heat, cover, and simmer 25 to 30 minutes until meat is tender.

4 Add pasta to sauce and stir to mix well. Serve from skillet.

PORK WITH SAUERKRAUT AND TOMATO

If you like the taste of caraway, you'll love this easy pork dinner.

12 oz pork tenderloin, trimmed of
    all fat and cut into 1-inch pieces

1/8 tsp black pepper

1 Tbsp canola oil

1 15-oz can low-sodium or regular tomato
    sauce

1 cup sauerkraut, well drained

1 1/2 tsp caraway seeds

1 Tbsp Splenda

1 cup brown or white rice, cooked
    according to package directions

PREP TIME: 10 MINUTES

SERVINGS: 4

SERVING SIZE: 1/4 RECIPE

Exchanges
2 1/2 Starch
1 Vegetable
2 Lean Meat

Calories 348
   Calories from Fat 72
Total Fat . . . . .8 g
   Saturated Fat . . . . . . .2 g
Cholesterol . . . . .55 mg
Sodium . . . . .291 mg
Total Carbohydrate . . . .46 g
   Dietary Fiber . . . . .4 g
   Sugars . . . . .1 g
Protein . . . . .23 g

1 Sprinkle the meat with pepper. In a large nonstick skillet over medium heat, brown the tenderloin pieces in oil, stirring frequently, about 5 to 7 minutes, until browned on all sides.

2 Meanwhile, in a small bowl, stir together the tomato sauce, sauerkraut, caraway seed, and Splenda. Add to the pan, and stir to coat the pork. Bring to a boil. Reduce heat, cover, and simmer about 10 to 12 minutes, stirring occasionally, until meat is cooked through.

3 Serve over rice.

Cajun Pork Chops

These quick pork chops are made with Cajun seasoning. We like the taste of our homemade seasoning (below). But you can substitute a commercial version if you like.

Cajun seasoning

    1 Tbsp paprika

1/4 tsp salt

1/2 Tbsp garlic powder

1/2 Tbsp onion powder

1/2 Tbsp dried oregano

1/2 Tbsp dried thyme leaves

1/4 tsp cayenne pepper

1/4 tsp black pepper

Pork chops

    3 cups frozen pepper and onion stir-fry

    2 Tbsp olive oil, divided

    4 6-oz thin-sliced bone-in pork chops, trimmed of fat

1/4 tsp salt

1/8 tsp black pepper

    1 15-oz can low-sodium or regular tomato sauce

1 1/2 tsp Cajun seasoning (see above)

    1 cup quick-cooking white rice, cooked according to package directions

Prep Time: 15 minutes

Servings: 4

Serving Size: 1 chop, plus 1/2 cup sauce and 3/4 cup rice

Exchanges
1 1/2 Starch
2 Vegetable
3 Lean Meat
1/2 Fat

Calories 367
   Calories from Fat . . .121
Total Fat . . . . .13 g
   Saturated Fat . . . . .4 g
Cholesterol . . . . .71 mg
Sodium . . . . .284 mg
Total Carbohydrate . . . .31 g
   Dietary Fiber . . . . .3 g
   Sugars . . . . .9 g
Protein . . . . .28 g

1 To prepare Cajun seasoning, mix together all ingredients in a small bowl. Store in a tightly capped jar.

2 In a large nonstick skillet over medium heat, cook the peppers and onions in 1 tablespoon of oil, stirring frequently until the onions are softened, about 5 or 6 minutes. Remove the mixture to a small bowl and reserve.

3 Sprinkle the pork chops with salt and pepper. In the skillet, over medium heat, brown the pork chops in oil, about 4 or 5 minutes, turning when one side is browned.

4 Add the tomato sauce, Cajun seasoning, and reserved peppers and onions, and stir. Bring to a boil. Reduce heat, cover, and simmer about 8 minutes, stirring occasionally.

5 Remove the lid, and raise heat to medium-high. Cook down sauce rapidly, stirring occasionally, until reduced by half, about 5 to 7 minutes.

6 Serve pork chops and sauce over rice.

PORK CHOP, CABBAGE, AND APPLE DINNER WITH CARAWAY

Pork chops, cabbage, and apples not only go together taste-wise, but they all cook quickly. This is a hearty and very savory quick-fix dinner.

3 Tbsp tomato ketchup

1 1/2 Tbsp lite soy sauce

2 tsp clover honey

1/2 tsp caraway seeds

4 4-oz boneless loin pork chops, trimmed of fat

1 Tbsp corn oil or canola oil

1 small onion, chopped

2 1/2 Tbsp orange juice or water

1 large Golden Delicious or other similar sweet apple (peeled or unpeeled), thinly sliced

4 cups very coarsely shredded cabbage

Salt and black pepper to taste (optional)

PREP TIME: 20 MINUTES

SERVINGS: 4

SERVING SIZE: 1 PORK CHOP AND ABOUT 2/3 CUP CABBAGE AND APPLES

Exchanges
3 Lean Meat
1 Vegetable
1 Fruit

Calories 256
   Calories from Fat 74
Total Fat . . . . .8 g
   Saturated Fat . . . . .1 g
Cholesterol . . . . .65 mg
Sodium . . . . .422 mg
Total Carbohydrate . . . .22 g
   Dietary Fiber . . . . .4 g
   Sugars . . . . .16 g
Protein . . . . .25 g

1 In a medium bowl, stir together the ketchup, soy sauce, honey, and caraway seeds. Add the chops, tossing until coated. Marinate for at least 5 minutes and preferably 10 minutes.

2 Combine the oil and onion in a 12-inch nonstick skillet over medium-high heat. Cook, stirring, until onions are softened and just beginning to brown, about 3 to 5 minutes.

3 Add the chops to the skillet, reserving the unabsorbed marinade in the bowl. Cook the chops, occasionally turning until well browned on both sides, until almost cooked through, about 10 to 12 minutes longer. (If the chops begin to dry out, add a few teaspoons of water to the skillet.) Remove the chops from the skillet and reserve.

4 Stir the orange juice into the reserved marinade. Add the marinade liquid, then the apples and cabbage, to the skillet, stirring until well mixed. Add salt and pepper to taste. Bring to a simmer over high heat. Adjust heat so the cabbage simmers gently and cooks down slightly, about 3 minutes.

5 Lay the chops over the cabbage. Continue cooking until the chops and cabbage are just cooked through, a few minutes longer. If the cabbage begins to stick to the pan, add a little more water. Add salt and pepper to taste.

HAM, ASPARAGUS, AND MUSHROOM STIR-FRY

This is a great way to take advantage of fresh asparagus when it's in season.

1 1/2 lb fresh asparagus

1/3 cup fat-free low-sodium or regular chicken broth

1 1/2 Tbsp lite soy sauce

2 tsp cornstarch

1 Tbsp peanut oil or corn oil

12 oz lean smoked ham, well trimmed and cut into scant 3/4-inch cubes

2 1/2 cups coarsely sliced mushrooms

1 medium onion, chopped

2 cups hot cooked brown or white rice for serving

PREP TIME: 20 MINUTES

SERVINGS: 4

SERVING SIZE: 1 CUP, PLUS 1/2 CUP COOKED RICE

Exchanges
1 1/2 Starch
3 Lean Meat
2 Vegetable

Calories 324
    Calories from Fat 86
Total Fat . . . . .10 g
    Saturated Fat . . . . .2 g
Cholesterol . . . . .48 mg
Sodium . . . . .1413 mg
Total Carbohydrate . . . .33 g
    Dietary Fiber . . . . .4 g
    Sugars . . . . .5 g
Protein . . . . .28 g

1 Break off the tough ends (about 3 or 4 inches) of the asparagus spears and discard. Cut the remainder of the spears on a diagonal into 1 1/4-inch pieces.

2 In a small bowl, stir together the chicken broth, soy sauce, and cornstarch until blended.

3 In a 12-inch or larger nonstick stir-fry pan or similar deep-sided skillet over medium-high heat, heat the oil to hot but not smoking. Add the ham, mushrooms, and onion and cook, stirring frequently, until the mushrooms exude their juices, about 5 minutes.

4 Add the asparagus and cook, stirring, 3 minutes longer.

5 Stir the chicken broth mixture. Add it to the skillet, stirring. Cook until the mixture thickens and becomes clear and the asparagus pieces are crisp-tender when tested with a fork, 2 or 3 minutes longer. Serve over the rice.

HAM AND "EGG" FRIED RICE SKILLET

More substantial and less oily than the fried rice offered in Chinese restaurants, this makes a very quick skillet meal. The egg in the recipe is actually egg substitute—both low in fat and cholesterol and also very convenient to use. Like regular Chinese fried rice, this dish calls for leftover cooked long grain rice—brown rice is more healthful, but white is more traditional.

1 1/2 Tbsp peanut oil or corn oil

4 or 5 medium green onions, including tender tops, coarsely sliced

2 medium celery stalks, coarsely chopped

2 medium carrots, chopped

1/4 cup fat-free low-sodium or regular chicken broth

3 Tbsp lite soy sauce

1/8 to 1/4 tsp black pepper, to taste

1 1/3 cups frozen (thawed) green peas

1 cup well-trimmed diced (1/4-inch) smoked ham

1 1/2 cups cooked leftover long-grain brown or white rice

1/2 cup liquid egg substitute

1/4 tsp salt (optional)

Prep Time: 20 minutes

Servings: 8

Serving Size: 1 cup

Exchanges
1 Starch
1 Vegetable
1 Lean Meat
1/2 Fat

Calories 180
    Calories from Fat 48
Total Fat . . . . .5 g
    Saturated Fat . . . . .1 g
Cholesterol . . . . .13 mg
Sodium . . . . .732 mg
Total Carbohydrate . . . .21 g
    Dietary Fiber . . . . . . .4 g
    Sugars . . . . .5 g
Protein . . . . .12 g

1 In a 12-inch nonstick skillet over medium-high heat, combine the oil, green onions, celery, and carrot. Cook the vegetables, stirring frequently, until the green onions begin to soften, 2 to 3 minutes.

2 Stir in the chicken broth, soy sauce, and black pepper. Bring to a simmer over medium-high heat; cook until the carrot is almost tender, about 3 minutes longer. Stir the peas, ham, and rice into the mixture; cook until heated through, 1 1/2 minutes longer.

3 Push the mixture to one side. Add the egg substitute to the skillet in a pool. Sprinkle with salt, if desired. Cook 2 1/2 minutes without stirring. Stir to redistribute the egg mixture, then cook about 2 minutes longer or until the egg mixture just sets. Scrape the egg from the skillet bottom, breaking it into bits; cook until it firms up slightly, about 30 seconds longer. Stir it into the fried rice mixture.

PORK AND VEGETABLE STIR-FRY WITH HOT CHILI PASTE

Pork tenderloin cubes, broccoli, and cauliflower are seasoned with commercial chili paste for an easy entree with appealing Asian flavor. Chili paste with garlic (also called chili puree with garlic) can be obtained with Chinese or Asian supplies in many supermarkets. Some brands are spicier than others, so start with 2 tablespoons of paste and add more if desired.

1 lb well-trimmed pork tenderloin, cut into 1-inch cubes

3 tsp corn oil or peanut oil, divided

1 small onion, chopped

1/3 cup coarsely diced red bell pepper (optional)

2 to 3 Tbsp chili paste (or puree) with garlic

1 1/2 Tbsp lite soy sauce

1 Tbsp cornstarch

1/2 cup cold water

2 cups medium broccoli florets

2 cups medium cauliflower florets

2 cups hot cooked long-grain brown or white rice

PREP TIME: 20 MINUTES

SERVINGS: 4

SERVING SIZE: 1 CUP PORK AND VEGETABLES, PLUS 1/2 CUP RICE

Exchanges
2 Starch
3 Lean Meat
1 Vegetable

Calories	331
Calories from Fat	78
Total Fat	9 g
Saturated Fat	2 g
Cholesterol	65 mg
Sodium	504 mg
Total Carbohydrate	35 g
Dietary Fiber	5 g
Sugars	7 g
Protein	29 g

1 Pat the pork cubes dry with paper towels. Heat 1 teaspoon oil to hot but not smoking in a 12-inch nonstick stir-fry pan or deep-sided skillet over medium-high heat. Add half the pork cubes and cook, turning, until browned all over and just cooked through, about 4 minutes. Remove the pork from the pan and reserve. Add 1 more teaspoon oil and heat to hot. Repeat browning with the remaining pork cubes. Remove the second batch of pork cubes and reserve with the first.

2 Add 1 more teaspoon oil to the skillet. Add the onions and bell peppers, if using, to the skillet. Continue cooking until the onions are soft and beginning to brown, about 3 minutes longer.

3 In a small non-reactive bowl, stir together 2 tablespoons chili paste with garlic, soy sauce, and cornstarch. Stir in cold water until very well blended. Add the chili paste mixture to the skillet; bring to a boil. Add the broccoli and cauliflower to the skillet. Cook, stirring, for 3 minutes longer.

4 Return the pork and any juices to the pan; cook just until the vegetables are crisp-tender and the pork cubes are just cooked through, about 2 minutes longer. If the mixture begins to boil dry, add a tablespoon or two more water as needed. Taste the dish and stir in up to an additional tablespoon of chili paste with garlic if desired. Serve over rice.

FRESH SALMON-POTATO SKILLET

For quickest preparation, you may want to buy boneless salmon pieces that are already cut into 4-ounce serving portions. However, salmon is usually more economical and easier to find sold in 1-pound filets (with skin on one side) that you cut into portions yourself. Many fish departments routinely remove the series of small lateral line bones along the thicker (head) end of these filets, but some markets don't. If you aren't sure, run your hand along the length of the fish about an inch below the upper edge to check. If any bone tips are protruding, either use a sharp paring knife and cut them out in a long, thin sliver, or pluck the bones out using tweezers or small pliers. Then, simply cut the fish crosswise into the 4-ounce portions called for.

1 Tbsp olive oil

1 small onion, chopped

2 medium celery stalks, chopped

2 1/2 cups 1/4 inch–thick slices red bliss or other thin-skinned boiling potatoes

1 cup fat-free low-sodium or regular chicken broth, divided

1 Tbsp Dijon or Dijon-style mustard

4 4-oz boneless salmon pieces, skin intact on one side

2 Tbsp chopped fresh parsley or chives

Salt and black pepper to taste (optional)

Lemon wedges for garnish

PREP TIME: 20 MINUTES

SERVINGS: 4

SERVING SIZE: 1 4-OZ SALMON PIECE, PLUS 2/3 CUP VEGETABLES

Exchanges
3 1/2 Starch
3 Lean Meat
1 Fat

Calories	326
Calories from Fat	117
Total Fat	13 g
Saturated Fat	1 g
Cholesterol	72 mg
Sodium	297 mg
Total Carbohydrate	24 g
Dietary Fiber	3 g
Sugars	2 g
Protein	27 g

1 In a 12-inch or similar nonstick skillet over medium-high heat, combine the oil, onion, and celery. Cook, stirring, until the onion begins to brown, 4 to 6 minutes.

2 Add the potato slices and 2/3 cup chicken broth to the skillet. Bring to a simmer; cook, uncovered, for 5 minutes.

3 Stir the remaining broth and mustard into the pan until smoothly incorporated. Push the potatoes to one side and add the salmon filets (skin side down), leaving a little space between them. Sprinkle the parsley or chives over top. Cover and simmer, stirring the potatoes once or twice, about 10 to 15 minutes or until the potatoes are barely tender and the salmon pieces look opaque in the thickest part when cut into with a small knife.

4 Add salt and pepper, if desired. Serve garnished with lemon wedges.

SHRIMP AND SCALLOPS, ASIAN STYLE

" In this recipe we use bottled, chopped ginger; it's in the dairy case at most grocery stores. "

1 Tbsp peanut oil

3 green onions, including green tops, thinly sliced

2 tsp chopped garlic

2 tsp minced bottled ginger

2 cups small broccoli florets

1 6-oz can sliced water chestnuts, drained

1/2 cup fat-free low-sodium or regular chicken broth

3 Tbsp lite soy sauce

3 Tbsp dry sherry

1/2 lb large fresh ready-to-cook shrimp

1/2 lb bay scallops, washed and cleaned

1 cup brown or long-grain white rice, cooked according to package directions

1 In a large nonstick skillet, combine the oil, green onions, garlic, and ginger. Add broccoli and water chestnuts. Cook over medium heat, stirring, until broccoli is crisp-tender, about 3 or 4 minutes.

2 Combine broth, soy sauce, and sherry in a small bowl. Add to pan. Bring to a boil. Add the shrimp and scallops. Reduce heat, and cook until scallops are just opaque, about 2 minutes. Serve mixture over rice.

PREP TIME: 15 MINUTES

SERVINGS: 4

SERVING SIZE: 1 CUP, PLUS 3/4 CUP RICE

Exchanges
2 1/2 Starch
2 Vegetable
2 Very Lean Meat
1/2 Fat

Calories 334
    Calories from Fat 52
Total Fat . . . . .6 g
    Saturated Fat . . . . .1 g
Cholesterol . . . . .102 mg
Sodium . . . . .712 mg
Total Carbohydrate . . . .46 g
    Dietary Fiber . . . . .4 g
    Sugars . . . . .6 g
Protein . . . . .22 g

MICROWAVE SPECIALS

QUICK BEEF AND BEAN CHILI

This easy chili is not too spicy, but not at all bland either. It's full of great flavors!

3/4 lb extra-lean ground beef round

1 large onion, finely chopped

2 large celery ribs, chopped

1 1/2 Tbsp mild to medium-hot chili powder

1 tsp dried thyme leaves

1/4 to 1/2 tsp cumin or caraway seeds

1/8 tsp salt or more to taste

1 28-oz can unsalted or reduced-sodium crushed tomatoes in juice

2 14 1/2-oz cans kidney beans, rinsed and drained

1 4-oz can chopped green chiles, drained

1 Combine the beef, onion, celery, chili powder, and dried thyme in a 2 1/2- to 3-quart glass casserole or similar microwave-safe dish, taking care to break up the beef as much as possible with a spoon. Cover with a plastic microwave cover or baking parchment and microwave on high power until the onion is limp, about 5 minutes, stopping and stirring after 2 minutes to break up the beef again.

2 Stir the cumin seeds (or caraway seeds), 1/8 teaspoon salt, tomatoes, kidney beans, and green chiles into the casserole. Re-cover the dish. Stirring every 2 minutes, microwave on high power, covered, for 8 to 12 minutes, or until the vegetables are tender and the flavors are blended. Taste and add more salt, if desired.

PREP TIME: 15 MINUTES

SERVINGS: 4 1/2

SERVING SIZE: 1 1/2 CUPS

Exchanges
2 1/2 Starch
2 Vegetable
2 Very Lean Meat

Calories 324
   Calories from Fat 36
Total Fat . . . . .4 g
   Saturated Fat . . . . . . .1 g
Cholesterol . . . . .40 mg
Sodium . . . . .601 mg
Total Carbohydrate . . . .45 g
   Dietary Fiber . . . . . . .17 g
   Sugars . . . . .8 g
Protein . . . . .27 g

Chicken-Vegetable Soup

When you want homemade chicken soup in a hurry, here's a quick and tasty version.

1 large skinless, boneless chicken breast half (about 3/4 lb)

1/4 cup chopped onion

1/8 tsp white pepper

1/2 tsp dried thyme leaves

3 1/2 cups fat-free low-sodium or regular chicken broth

1 bay leaf

1 1/2 cups frozen mixed vegetables

1/2 cup cooked brown rice or 1/4 cup quick-cooking rice

Prep Time: 8 minutes

Servings: 5

Serving Size: 1 cup

Exchanges
1/2 Starch
1 Vegetable
2 Very Lean Meat

Calories 134
  Calories from Fat 11
Total Fat . . . . .1 g
  Saturated Fat . . . . .0 g
Cholesterol . . . . .38 mg
Sodium . . . . .418 mg
Total Carbohydrate . . . .11 g
  Dietary Fiber . . . . .2 g
  Sugars . . . . .3 g
Protein . . . . .19 g

1 Cut the chicken into three large pieces. Combine the pieces and the chopped onion in a 2 1/2-quart microwave-safe casserole. Sprinkle with pepper and thyme. Cover with the casserole lid, and microwave on high power 4 to 5 minutes, turning the chicken over once, until it is cooked through.

2 With a fork, remove the chicken from the casserole. When chicken is cool enough to handle, carefully cut it into bite-sized pieces.

3 Return the chicken to the casserole. Add the chicken broth, bay leaf, vegetables, and rice. Cover with the casserole lid, and microwave on high power 4 to 5 minutes, stirring once or twice, until the vegetables are cooked through.

FLORENTINE CHICKEN SOUP

Here's an easy variation on the chicken soup theme.

1 large skinless, boneless
  chicken breast half (about 3/4 lb)

1/4 cup chopped onion

Pinch black pepper

1 tsp dried basil leaves

1 15-oz can stewed tomatoes

1 1/2 cups fat-free low-sodium or regular
  chicken broth

1 cup frozen loose-leaf spinach

1 bay leaf

1/2 cup cooked brown rice or 1/4 cup quick-
  cooking rice

PREP TIME: 8 MINUTES

SERVINGS: 5

SERVING SIZE: 1 CUP

Exchanges
1/2 Starch
2 Very Lean Meat
1 Vegetable

Calories 137
  Calories from Fat 12
Total Fat . . . . .1 g
  Saturated Fat . . . . .0 g
Cholesterol . . . . .38 mg
Sodium . . . . .450 mg
Total Carbohydrate . . . .13 g
  Dietary Fiber . . . . .2 g
  Sugars . . . . .3 g
Protein . . . . .19 g

1 Cut the chicken into three large pieces. Combine the pieces and the chopped onion in a 2 1/2-quart microwave-safe casserole. Sprinkle with pepper and basil. Cover with the casserole lid, and microwave on high power 4 to 5 minutes, turning the chicken over once, until it is cooked through.

2 With a fork, remove the chicken from the casserole. When the chicken is cool enough to handle, carefully cut it into bite-sized pieces.

3 Return the chicken to the casserole. Add the stewed tomatoes, chicken broth, spinach, bay leaf, and rice. Cover with the casserole lid, and microwave on high power 7 to 9 minutes, stirring once or twice, until the vegetables and rice are cooked through. Remove from microwave, and allow to sit 2 or 3 minutes.

SMOKED TURKEY AND JACK CHEESE QUESADILLAS

This is a light yet satisfying meal in a hurry. We like to serve the quesadillas with carrot and celery sticks.

4 *8-inch diameter flour tortillas*

2/3 *cup shredded, fat-free Monterey Jack cheese, jalapeno-flavored jack cheese, or fat-free cheddar cheese, divided*

1/4 *cup chopped, canned mild green chiles or coarsely chopped bottled roasted red sweet pepper, well drained, divided*

1/3 *cup diced (1/4-inch) fresh tomato*

4 to 6 *large very thin slices (about 5 oz) smoked lean turkey breast*

PREP TIME: 5 MINUTES

SERVINGS: 2

SERVING SIZE:
   1 QUESADILLA

Exchanges
2 1/2 Starch
1 Vegetable
4 Very Lean Meat

Calories 342
   Calories from Fat 18
Total Fat . . . . .2 g
   Saturated Fat . . . . .0 g
Cholesterol . . . . .63 mg
Sodium . . . . .740 mg
Total Carbohydrate . . . .43 g
   Dietary Fiber . . . . .4 g
   Sugars . . . . .2 g
Protein . . . . .38 g

1 Lay a tortilla on a microwave-safe plate. Sprinkle the tortilla evenly with 1/4 of the cheese. Cover the plate with a plastic microwave cover. Microwave on 50 percent power for 1 minute. If the cheese isn't partially melted, continue microwaving on 50 percent power just until it partially melts, stopping and checking every 30 seconds.

2 Spread half the green chiles (or red sweet peppers) and half the tomato over the cheese (or sprinkle the green pepper over the melted cheese). Lay half the turkey slices over the top, pressing down lightly. Sprinkle 1/4 of the cheese over the turkey. Cover the cheese with a second tortilla.

3 Return the quesadilla to the microwave oven. Cover with a plastic microwave cover. Microwave on 50 percent power for 1 minute. Lift the edge of the tortilla to see if the cheese is melted; if not, continue microwaving, checking every 20 seconds until the cheese is melted.

4 Repeat the assembly and microwaving process for the second quesadilla. Cut the quesadillas into wedges and serve.

SPICY BEEF AND PASTA CASSEROLE

" The blend of spices gives this casserole a rich flavor. The microwave speeds the preparation. "

1 1/2 cups uncooked fusilli, or other
    similar pasta shape

1 lb ground beef round

2 cups chopped cabbage

1 large onion, finely chopped

1 green bell pepper, seeded and chopped

1 14 1/2-oz can low-sodium or regular
    chopped tomatoes

1 8-oz can low-sodium or regular tomato
    sauce

1 1/2 tsp dried thyme leaves

1 tsp Dijon-style mustard

1/2 tsp ground cinnamon

1/4 tsp ground cloves

1/4 tsp ground black pepper

1/2 tsp salt, or to taste (optional)

PREP TIME: 15 MINUTES

SERVINGS: 6

SERVING SIZE: 1 CUP

Exchanges
1 Starch
2 Very Lean Meat
2 Vegetable

Calories 210
    Calories from Fat 26
Total Fat . . . . .3 g
    Saturated Fat . . . . . . .1 g
Cholesterol . . . . .38 mg
Sodium . . . . .77 mg
Total Carbohydrate . . . .26 g
    Dietary Fiber . . . . . . .3 g
    Sugars . . . . .8 g
Protein . . . . .20 g

1 Cook pasta according to package directions. Rinse and drain in a colander.

2 Meanwhile, in a 3-quart microwave-proof casserole, stir together the ground round, cabbage, onion, and green pepper. Cover with the casserole lid, and microwave on high power 7 to 9 minutes, stirring meat and breaking it up 1 or 2 times during microwaving, until the meat is cooked through. With a large spoon, break up any remaining large pieces of meat.

3 Stir in the tomatoes, tomato sauce, thyme, mustard, cinnamon, cloves, black pepper, and salt, if desired.

4 Cover with the casserole lid, and microwave on high power 5 to 6 minutes longer, stirring once during microwaving. Add the pasta. Microwave an additional 4 to 6 minutes on high power, turning the casserole 1/4 turn and stirring the contents once, until the cabbage is tender and the flavors are well blended.

Macaroni Lasagna

Much faster than usual versions, this remarkably savory microwave lasagna is made with leftover macaroni, rigatoni, or other pasta rather than with lasagna noodles. We like to cook extra pasta just so we'll have some on hand to make this easy entree. Although it is traditional to use ricotta cheese in lasagna, we prefer low-fat (but not salt-free) cottage cheese in this recipe. Note that you can omit the ham or pepperoni for a vegetarian dish.

1 6-oz package fresh, ready-to-use baby spinach leaves

1 1/2 tsp olive oil

1 small onion, chopped

1 cup chopped mushrooms

2 Tbsp finely chopped lean ham, or 1 1/2 Tbsp finely chopped pepperoni (optional)

1 1/2 cups 1 percent fat cottage cheese (not salt-free), preferably small curd

2/3 cup fine, dry bread crumbs, preferably whole wheat

1/4 cup liquid egg substitute (or 1 egg)

1/3 cup grated Parmesan cheese, divided

1 26-oz jar low-sodium spaghetti sauce or herb-seasoned pasta sauce

2 cups cooked medium-sized macaroni, rigatoni, or similar pasta (4 oz uncooked)

1 1/2 cups (about 6 oz) shredded or grated fat-free mozzarella cheese

PREP TIME: 20 MINUTES

SERVINGS: 6

SERVING SIZE:
1/6 CASSEROLE

Exchanges
2 1/2 Starch
2 Vegetable
2 1/2 Lean Meat

Calories 398
   Calories from Fat 90
Total Fat . . . . .10 g
   Saturated Fat . . . . .2 g
Cholesterol . . . . .11 mg
Sodium . . . . .662 mg
Total Carbohydrate . . . .50 g
   Dietary Fiber . . . . .6 g
   Sugars . . . . .18 g
Protein . . . . .27 g

1 Put the spinach in a large microwave-safe bowl. Cover with a plastic microwave-safe cover or baking parchment. Microwave on high power 1 1/2 to 2 minutes, or until the spinach is just tender. Turn it out into a colander to drain and cool. Meanwhile, combine the oil, onion, mushrooms, and ham or pepperoni (if using) in the same bowl. Microwave, covered, on high power for 2 minutes, stopping and stirring halfway through.

2 Squeeze the spinach completely dry with your hands. Coarsely chop it. Stir into the vegetable mixture until evenly incorporated. Re-cover and microwave on high power about 2 to 3 minutes longer, stopping and stirring at 1-minute intervals, until the vegetables are just tender.

3 Thoroughly stir the cottage cheese, bread crumbs, egg substitute (or egg), and half the Parmesan cheese into the vegetables until well blended.

4 Pour 1/2 cup spaghetti sauce into a 7- × 11-inch or 9-inch square microwave-safe dish. Arrange half the pasta over the sauce. Top with 3/4 cup mozzarella cheese, then another 1/2 cup sauce. Top with the cottage cheese mixture, spreading it out evenly. Top with another 1/2 cup sauce, then the remaining half of the pasta, remaining 3/4 cup mozzarella, and remaining sauce.

5 Re-cover the dish and microwave on high power for 8 to 12 minutes longer, until the mixture is bubbly at the edges and piping hot in the center. Uncover and sprinkle with the remaining Parmesan cheese. Let stand 10 to 15 minutes to firm up before serving.

6 Cut the lasagna into portions. It will be slightly soft, so carefully transfer it to plates using a wide-bladed spatula or two smaller spatulas.

Taco Casserole "Bake"

This is reminiscent of traditional taco salad, except that the filling is readied in a casserole and "baked" in a microwave oven.

2 tsp olive oil

1 small onion, chopped

3/4 cup chopped celery

1/2 lb extra-lean ground beef round

1 or 2 tsp mild to hot chili powder, as desired

1 14 to 15 1/2-oz can kidney beans, rinsed and drained

1/3 cup mild to medium-hot salsa or picante sauce

1 4-oz can chopped mild green chiles, well drained (optional)

TOPPINGS

2 cups broken-up baked (low-fat) tortilla chips

2/3 cup shredded or grated fat-free cheddar or Monterey Jack cheese for garnish

2 1/2 cups cored and diced tomatoes

2 1/2 cups shredded iceberg lettuce or other crisp lettuce

PREP TIME: 20 MINUTES

SERVINGS: 5

SERVING SIZE:
   1/5 CASSEROLE,
   1/5 TOPPINGS

Exchanges
1 Starch
1/2 Fruit
3 Lean Meat

Calories 328
   Calories from Fat 72
Total Fat . . . . .8 g
   Saturated Fat . . . . .2 g
Cholesterol . . . . .27 mg
Sodium . . . . .695 mg
Total Carbohydrate . . . .42 g
   Dietary Fiber . . . . .8 g
   Sugars . . . . .7 g
Protein . . . . .22 g

1 Combine the oil, onion, and celery in a 9 1/2-inch round deep-dish glass pie plate or similar microwave-safe dish. Cover with a plastic microwave-safe cover or baking parchment and microwave on high power for 3 minutes, stopping and stirring halfway through.

2 Stir in the beef, breaking it up with a spoon. Stir in the chili powder. Re-cover the dish. Microwave on high power, stopping and breaking up the beef at 30-second intervals, until no pinkness remains, 3 to 4 minutes longer.

3 Partially mash the beans with a fork. Stir the beans, salsa, and green chiles (if using) into the beef mixture. Then, spread the mixture out evenly in the dish. Re-cover the dish. Microwave on high power for 3 to 4 minutes longer, until the edges are bubbling and the casserole is piping hot in the center.

4 To serve, place some chips, then the portions of the beef-bean mixture on plates. Top the servings with more chips, the cheese, tomato, and lettuce; serve immediately.

Hurry-Up Spaghetti Casserole "Bake"

This is a real family pleaser. It's a good way to use up leftover spaghetti.

1 1/2 tsp olive oil

1 medium onion, chopped

1 medium (6-inch) zucchini, chopped

1/2 lb extra-lean ground beef round

1 1/4 tsp dried oregano leaves

1/8 tsp dried hot red pepper flakes, optional

2 cups bottled tomato-herb pasta sauce (with garlic, oregano, or other Italian-style herbs)

1 8-oz can no-salt-added tomato sauce

1 7-oz jar roasted red sweet peppers, drained and chopped

3 3/4 cups leftover cooked whole-wheat or regular spaghetti, linguini, or similar pasta, cut into 4-inch lengths

2/3 cup fat-free shredded or coarsely grated mozzarella, Colby, or other mild cheese

PREP TIME: 15 MINUTES

SERVINGS: 5

SERVING SIZE: 1 1/2 CUPS

Exchanges
3 Starch
2 Vegetable
1 1/2 Lean Meat

Calories 378
   Calories from Fat 54
Total Fat . . . . .6 g
   Saturated Fat . . . . .2 g
Cholesterol . . . . .27 mg
Sodium . . . . .875 mg
Total Carbohydrate . . . .57 g
   Dietary Fiber . . . . . . .9 g
   Sugars . . . . .13 g
Protein . . . . .24 g

1 Combine the oil, onion, and zucchini in a 4-quart (or similar) microwave-safe round dish. Cover with a microwave-safe cover or baking parchment and microwave on high power until the onion is limp, about 3 minutes, stopping and stirring several times.

2 Stir in the beef, breaking it up with a spoon. Stir in the oregano and red pepper flakes. Re-cover the dish, and microwave on high power until the beef is no longer pink, about 3 minutes longer, stopping and breaking up any clumps of beef several times.

3 Stir in the pasta sauce, tomato sauce, and roasted peppers. Re-cover the dish and microwave on high power until the sauce is bubbling at the edges, about 7 to 9 minutes longer.

4 Thoroughly stir the pasta into the sauce until evenly incorporated. Re-cover the dish and microwave on high power until the dish is piping hot throughout, about 4 minutes longer. Stir well. Top the casserole with the cheese; re-cover the dish and let stand a minute or two until the cheese begins to melt. Serve immediately.

ITALIAN SAUSAGE AND VEGGIES MICROWAVE "SKILLET"

Sausage—even the reduced-fat turkey sausage called for here—isn't super-lean, but it is quite flavorful so a little can go a long way. This simple dish is tasty and satisfying.

2 *large red bliss or other thin-skinned boiling potatoes*

1/2 *lb hot Italian turkey sausage in casings*

1 *medium onion, chopped*

1 *large celery rib, chopped*

2 1/2 *cups frozen (thawed) mixed red, green, and yellow bell pepper strips, very well drained*

Pinch *dried hot red pepper flakes*

1/4 *tsp salt (optional)*

1 *14 1/2-oz can diced tomatoes (plain or with Italian seasonings) or reduced-sodium diced tomatoes*

2/3 *cup canned garbanzo beans, thoroughly rinsed and drained*

PREP TIME: 15 MINUTES

SERVINGS: 4

SERVING SIZE: 1 1/2 CUPS

Exchanges
2 Starch
1 Vegetable
1 Medium-Fat Meat

Calories 279
  Calories from Fat 63
Total Fat . . . . .7 g
  Saturated Fat . . . . .0 g
Cholesterol . . . . .34 mg
Sodium . . . . .506 mg
Total Carbohydrate . . . .39 g
  Dietary Fiber . . . . .7 g
  Sugars . . . . .7 g
Protein . . . . .15 g

1 Puncture each potato all the way through with a skewer or thin-bladed paring knife. Place on a microwave-safe dish; cover loosely with wax paper. Microwave the potatoes on high power for 5 to 7 minutes or until just tender when poked with a skewer (or knife) in the thickest part. Set aside to cool while the remaining ingredients are prepared.

2 Slit the sausage casings and scrape out the sausage into a 2 1/2- to 3-quart oven-proof glass casserole or similar microwave-safe dish. Stir in the onion and celery, taking care to break up the sausage as much as possible with a spoon. Cover with a plastic microwave-safe cover or baking parchment, and microwave on high power until the onion is limp, about 5 minutes, stopping and stirring at 2-minute intervals to break up the sausage as much as possible.

3 Stir the bell peppers, pepper flakes, 1/4 teaspoon salt (if using), and tomatoes into the casserole. Re-cover the dish. Stirring every 2 minutes, microwave on high power, covered, for 6 to 8 minutes, or until the vegetables are tender and the flavors are blended.

4 Coarsely cube the potatoes. Stir them and the garbanzo beans into the sausage mixture. Re-cover the dish; microwave on high power just until piping hot, about 2 minutes longer. Taste and add more salt, if desired.

Shrimp Risotto with Vegetables

"The rice used in risotto, called Arborio rice, is very absorbent and starchy, which accounts for its creamy, almost pudding-like consistency. Arborio rice is sold in gourmet shops, the gourmet sections of some supermarkets, and ethnic Italian markets. Unlike most risottos, microwave versions don't need constant stirring during cooking. This one has a savory flavor that complements the shrimp nicely."

1 Tbsp olive oil, preferably extra-virgin

3/4 cup finely chopped onions

2 large garlic cloves, peeled and minced

2 cups diced celery

1/2 cup finely diced carrot

3/4 cup Arborio rice

2 3/4 cups fat-free low-sodium or regular to 3 1/4 chicken broth

1 7-oz jar roasted red sweet peppers, well drained and chopped

1/4 cup oil-packed, sun-dried tomatoes, drained and chopped

3/4 lb peeled and cooked frozen shrimp, thawed

1/4 cup freshly grated Parmesan cheese

PREP TIME: 25 MINUTES

SERVINGS: 6

SERVING SIZE: 1 CUP

Exchanges
1 Starch
1 Vegetable
2 Very Lean Meat
1/2 Fat

Calories 208
    Calories from Fat 43
Total Fat . . . . .5 g
    Saturated Fat . . . . .1 g
Cholesterol . . . . .113 mg
Sodium . . . . .527 mg
Total Carbohydrate . . . .24 g
    Dietary Fiber . . . . .2 g
    Sugars . . . . .4 g
Protein . . . . .17 g

1 In a 2-quart (or similar) round microwave-safe casserole dish, stir together the olive oil, onions, garlic, celery, and carrot. Cover the dish with a plastic microwave-safe cover or wax paper. Microwave, on high power, stopping and stirring after each minute until the onion is translucent and softened, 2 1/2 to 3 minutes. Stir the rice into the vegetable mixture and microwave on high power, uncovered, for 1 1/2 minutes longer.

2 Stir in 2 3/4 cups chicken broth. Re-cover the casserole, and microwave the mixture on high power for 10 minutes, stopping and stirring after 5 minutes.

3 Stir in the roasted red peppers and sun-dried tomatoes until evenly incorporated. Continue microwaving on high, loosely covered, for 8 to 10 minutes longer, or until the rice is almost tender and most of the liquid is absorbed, but the mixture is still slightly moist and soupy. (If the mixture is firm and dry rather than slightly soupy, stir in up to 1/2 cup more broth.)

4 Stir the shrimp into the mixture. Microwave, covered, on 50 percent power until the shrimp are just heated through, about 2 minutes longer. Stir well.

5 Sprinkle with Parmesan cheese and serve.

ITALIAN CASSEROLE

Here's a quick, easy, and tasty Italian-style casserole. The dish is one of the favorite meals we serve to vegetarian friends. Be sure to use dry-pack frozen spinach—the kind that comes in a bag and is easy to separate.

1 cup uncooked medium pasta shells

1 15-oz carton low-fat ricotta cheese (1 gram saturated fat per 1/4 cup)

1 1/2 cups fat-free shredded mozzarella cheese

1/4 cup grated Parmesan cheese, divided

1 1/2 cups frozen loose-leaf spinach (thawed)

1 Tbsp instant minced onion

1 tsp minced garlic

1/4 tsp salt, or to taste (optional)

2 cups low-fat low-sodium spaghetti sauce

1 15 1/2-oz can chickpeas, rinsed and drained

PREP TIME: 20 MINUTES

SERVINGS: 5

SERVING SIZE: 1/5 CASSEROLE

Exchanges
3 Starch
2 Vegetable
2 Lean Meat

Calories 357
   Calories from Fat 45
Total Fat . . . . .5 g
   Saturated Fat . . . . . . .2 g
Cholesterol . . . . .22 mg
Sodium . . . . .744 mg
Total Carbohydrate . . . .51 g
   Dietary Fiber . . . . .6 g
   Sugars . . . . .8 g
Protein . . . . .27 g

1 Cook pasta according to package directions without added salt or fat. Drain and reserve.

2 In a large bowl, stir together the ricotta and mozzarella cheese, 2 tablespoons of the Parmesan cheese, spinach, onion, garlic, and salt, if desired. Carefully stir in the pasta shells, being careful not to break them up.

3 In a medium-sized bowl, stir together the spaghetti sauce and chickpeas.

4 Layer half the cheese mixture in a deep 2-quart microwave-safe casserole. Spoon on half the tomato sauce mixture. Spoon on the remaining cheese mixture. Top with the remaining sauce mixture. Sprinkle with the remaining Parmesan cheese.

5 Microwave, covered, 7 or 8 minutes at high power until the mixture is bubbly.

Tex-Mex Veggie, Bean, and Rice con Queso Dinner

If you are serving this dish to vegetarians, use vegetable broth rather than chicken broth in the recipe.

1 Tbsp olive oil

3 or 4 green onions, including tender tops, chopped

1 cup fat-free low-sodium chicken broth or vegetable broth

2 tsp mild to medium-hot chili powder, as desired

1 tsp dried oregano leaves

1 cup quick-cooking white rice

1 14-oz package frozen (thawed) corn, black bean, bell pepper, and celery medley, or a similar corn and bean frozen vegetable medley

Scant 1/2 cup mild to medium-hot salsa or picante sauce

4 oz (about 1 cup lightly packed) shredded reduced-fat cheddar cheese or Monterey Jack cheese

1/4 cup chopped cilantro leaves for garnish (optional)

PREP TIME: 20 MINUTES

SERVINGS: 4

SERVING SIZE: 1 1/4 CUPS (1/4 CASSEROLE)

Exchanges
2 Starch
1 Vegetable
1 Medium-Fat Meat
1 Fat

Calories	.310
Calories from Fat	.84
Total Fat	.9 g
Saturated Fat	.4 g
Cholesterol	.20 mg
Sodium	.525 mg
Total Carbohydrate	.36 g
Dietary Fiber	.7 g
Sugars	.5 g
Protein	.15 g

1 Combine the oil and green onions in a 9 1/2-inch deep-dish glass pie plate or a 9-inch square glass dish (or other similar microwave-safe dish). Cover with a plastic microwave cover or wax paper. Microwave on high power, stopping and stirring after 2 minutes, until the green onions are limp, about 3 minutes.

2 Stir in the broth, chili powder, and oregano. Microwave, uncovered, on high power until the broth is hot, about 3 minutes longer.

3 Stir in the rice. Re-cover the dish and microwave on high power for 3 minutes. Stir in the vegetable medley and salsa; re-cover. Stopping and stirring after 3 minutes, continue microwaving on high power for 5 to 8 minutes longer or until the rice and vegetables are just tender.

4 Sprinkle the cheese over the dish. Return to the microwave oven and microwave, uncovered, on high power until the cheese partially melts, 1 to 2 minutes longer. Garnish with cilantro leaves, if desired.

SLOW-COOKER MEALS

CHICKEN CREOLE

Use large chicken breasts for this Creole-inspired recipe, as small breasts will cook too quickly.

2 cups fat-free low-sodium or regular chicken broth

1 15-oz can low-sodium or regular tomato sauce

2 cups frozen (thawed onion) onion-pepper stir-fry

2 cups coarsely chopped cabbage

1 green bell pepper, seeded and diced

2 tsp minced garlic

1 large bay leaf

1 tsp paprika

2 tsp dried marjoram

1 tsp dried thyme leaves

1/4 tsp salt, or to taste (optional)

1/4 tsp black pepper, or to taste (optional)

2 large, bone-in chicken breast halves, skin and fat removed

1/2 cup uncooked long-grain white rice

PREP TIME: 15 MINUTES

SERVINGS: 5

SERVING SIZE: 1 CUP

Exchanges
1 Starch
2 Lean Meat
2 Vegetable

Calories 201
    Calories from Fat 12
Total Fat . . . . .1 g
    Saturated Fat . . . . .0 g
Cholesterol . . . . .38 mg
Sodium . . . . .277 mg
Total Carbohydrate . . . .27 g
    Dietary Fiber . . . . . . .3 g
    Sugars . . . . .9 g
Protein . . . . .19 g

1 In a 2 1/2-quart or larger slow cooker, combine the chicken broth and tomato sauce. Add onion-pepper stir-fry, cabbage, green bell pepper, garlic, bay leaf, paprika, marjoram, thyme, salt, and black pepper, if desired. Stir to mix well. Add chicken and rice. Cover and cook on high 1 hour.

2 Stir the chicken and vegetables down into the sauce. Reduce the heat to low, and cook an additional 5 or 6 hours. Or cook at high heat an additional 2 or 3 hours. Remove the bay leaf. Remove the chicken. When cool enough to handle, cut into slices and discard bones. Return chicken to pot.

CURRIED CHICKEN AND PEANUT SOUP

" If you like peanuts, you'll appreciate the flavor of this unusual soup. The peanuts provide a nice crunch. "

1 cup dry-roasted unsalted
   or salted peanuts

5 cups fat-free low-sodium or
   regular chicken broth

2 large bone-in chicken breast halves, skin
   and fat removed

2 cups thinly sliced cabbage

1/4 cup uncooked basmati rice

1 medium onion, chopped

1 1/2 tsp minced garlic

12 baby carrots

2 celery stalks, sliced

1 Tbsp mild curry powder

1 1/2 tsp dried thyme leaves

1 tsp ground cumin

Salt and pepper to taste (optional)

PREP TIME: 20 MINUTES

SERVINGS: 10

SERVING SIZE: 1 CUP

Exchanges
1 Carbohydrate
1 Very Lean Meat
1 1/2 Fat

Calories 166
   Calories from Fat 72
Total Fat . . . . .8 g
   Saturated Fat . . . . . . .2 g
Cholesterol . . . . .19 mg
Sodium . . . . .289 mg
Total Carbohydrate . . . .12 g
   Dietary Fiber . . . . . . .3 g
   Sugars . . . . .3 g
Protein . . . . .14 g

1 Coarsely chop the peanuts in a food processor, using 8 to 10 on/off bursts.

2 In a 3-quart or larger slow cooker, combine the peanuts, broth, chicken, cabbage, rice, onion, garlic, carrots, celery, curry powder, thyme, and cumin.

3 Cover and cook on high heat 1 hour. Reduce the heat, and cook for 4 1/2 to 5 1/2 hours on low heat. Add salt and pepper to taste, if desired.

4 Remove the chicken from the pot with a slotted spoon. When the chicken is cool enough to handle, remove meat from bone and cut it into pieces. Return the meat to the pot.

TURKEY-VEGETABLE STEW

"Turkey wings are perfect for the slow cooker because they need to be cooked for a long time to become tender. They also have a lot of flavor and make a very tasty stew. (Note that the stew will not seem to have enough liquid at first, but will become much juicier as the vegetables cook down.)"

2 1/2 *lbs turkey wings*

   2 *chicken bouillon cubes or*
   2 *tsp granules dissolved in 1 1/2 cups*
   hot water

1/3 *cup chopped fresh parsley leaves*

3/4 *tsp dried thyme leaves*

3/4 *tsp dried basil leaves*

1/4 *tsp black pepper, or to taste*

   2 *medium onions, cut into eighths*

   3 *medium carrots, cut crosswise into*
   1-inch lengths

   2 *medium celery stalks, cut crosswise into*
   3/4-inch pieces

   1 *cup rutabaga or turnip chunks (about*
   3/4-inch pieces)

   2 *large thin-skinned potatoes, cut into*
   1-inch chunks

1/4 *tsp salt (optional)*

PREP TIME: 25 MINUTES

SERVINGS: 7

SERVING SIZE: 1 CUP

Exchanges
1 Starch
1 Lean Meat
2 Vegetable

Calories 189
  Calories from Fat 20
Total Fat . . . . .2 g
  Saturated Fat . . . . . . .1 g
Cholesterol . . . . .58 mg
Sodium . . . . .336 mg
Total Carbohydrate . . . .22 g
  Dietary Fiber . . . . . . .4 g
  Sugars . . . . .6 g
Protein . . . . .20 g

1 Trim off and discard any loose skin from the turkey wings; don't worry about removing it from the wing tips and other areas where it is difficult to peel away.

2 In a 3-quart or larger slow cooker, combine the bouillon-water mixture, parsley, thyme, basil, and black pepper. Add the turkey wings, pushing them down into the liquid. In the order listed, top with the onions, carrots, celery, rutabaga, and potatoes, sprinkling each layer with a little of the salt (if using). A 3-quart cooker will be full.

3 Cover and cook on the high setting for 5 hours and up to 7 hours, if desired. (If possible, turn the setting to low after 5 hours if cooking any longer.)

4 Remove the turkey wings; set aside until cool enough to handle. Remove the meat from the turkey wings in chunks. Skim excess fat from the surface of the stew. Return the meat to the pot; stir to mix the ingredients. Reheat the turkey until hot. Add more pepper and add salt to taste, if desired.

TURKEY-BARLEY-VEGETABLE SOUP

"Old-fashioned, home-style flavor makes this simple soup appealing. It's a good, simple meal to come home to at the end of a busy day."

2 1/2 lbs turkey wings

1/2 cup pearl barley

4 cups fat-free low-sodium or regular chicken broth

3/4 tsp dried marjoram leaves

3/4 tsp dried thyme leaves

1/2 tsp black pepper

2 medium onions, coarsely chopped

2 medium carrots, very coarsely diced

1 1/2 cups or 1 10-oz package frozen (thawed) corn kernels or succotash

1/2 cup chopped celery

1 14 1/2-oz can diced tomatoes, including juice

Salt to taste

PREP TIME: 25 MINUTES

SERVINGS: 10

SERVING SIZE: 1 CUP

Exchanges
1 Starch
1 Lean Meat
1 Vegetable

Calories 144
   Calories from Fat 16
Total Fat . . . . .2 g
   Saturated Fat . . . . .0 g
Cholesterol . . . . .41 mg
Sodium . . . . .326 mg
Total Carbohydrate . . . .17 g
   Dietary Fiber . . . . .3 g
   Sugars . . . . .5 g
Protein . . . . .16 g

1 Trim off and discard as much loose skin as possible from the turkey wings; don't worry about removing it from the wing tips and other areas where it is difficult to peel away.

2 In a 3-quart or larger slow cooker, combine the barley, broth, marjoram, thyme, and pepper. Top with the turkey wings, onions, carrots, corn, and celery. Turn on the high setting, and cook at least 45 minutes and, if possible, 1 hour. Turn to the low setting, and cook for at least 8 hours and up to 12 hours, if desired.

3 Remove the turkey wings from the pot and set aside until cool enough to handle. Meanwhile, stir the tomatoes into the pot, and continue cooking. Remove the meat from the turkey wings in bite-size pieces. Stir the turkey meat into the soup. Heat it until piping hot. Add salt to taste.

BARBECUED BEEF AND VEGETABLE STEW

This is a tangy, robust-tasting stew, and it is easy and convenient, too. Don't worry that there doesn't seem to be enough liquid when you start the cooker. The vegetables and meat cook down and release their juices, providing plenty of liquid at the end.

1 1/2 lb beef top round steak, trimmed of fat and cut into 1-inch pieces

1/2 cup barbecue sauce

1 Tbsp clover honey or packed light brown sugar

2 beef bouillon cubes or 2 tsp beef bouillon granules, dissolved in 1/2 cup hot water

1 tsp ground allspice

4 medium onions, quartered

4 large carrots, cut crosswise into 1-inch pieces

2 cups frozen (thawed) cut green beans

2 large celery stalks, cut crosswise into 1-inch pieces

4 medium red bliss or other thin-skinned potatoes (unpeeled), cut into 1-inch chunks

Salt and black pepper (optional)

PREP TIME: 25 MINUTES

SERVINGS: 9

SERVING SIZE: 1 CUP

Exchanges
1 Starch
1 Lean Meat
3 Vegetable

Calories	.225
Calories from Fat	..28
Total Fat	.3 g
Saturated Fat	.1 g
Cholesterol	.43 mg
Sodium	.388 mg
Total Carbohydrate	.30 g
Dietary Fiber	.5 g
Sugars	.11 g
Protein	.21 g

1 Combine the beef, barbecue sauce, honey, bouillon-water mixture, and allspice in a 3-quart or larger slow cooker. Stir well to blend.

2 In the order called for, top the beef with the onions, carrots, green beans, celery, and potatoes; press down each layer slightly, and, if desired, very lightly sprinkle each vegetable layer with salt and pepper as you add it. (If you are using a 3-quart cooker it will be full.)

3 Turn the cooker setting on high. Cover and cook at least 5 hours and up to 10 hours, until the beef is very tender and the vegetables are cooked through when tested with a fork. Stir well and ladle into soup plates.

TANGY BEEF SOUP

Long cooking is the secret of success in this hearty soup. We've found that just a little bit of rice thickens the whole pot.

> 1 large onion, finely chopped
>
> 2 tsp minced garlic
>
> 2 cups thinly sliced cabbage
>
> 2 cups frozen (thawed) petite green beans
>
> 10 baby carrots
>
> 2 Tbsp uncooked long-grain white rice
>
> 1 lb beef round, trimmed of all fat and cut into small bite-sized pieces
>
> 2 1/2 cups defatted beef broth or bouillon
>
> 1 15-oz can low-sodium or regular tomato sauce
>
> 1 Tbsp sugar
>
> 1/2 Tbsp apple cider vinegar
>
> 1 1/2 tsp dried thyme leaves
>
> 1 tsp Dijon-style mustard
>
> 1/4 tsp black pepper

PREP TIME: 15 MINUTES

SERVINGS: 8

SERVING SIZE: 1 CUP

Exchanges
1 Lean Meat
3 Vegetable

Calories 146
  Calories from Fat 31
Total Fat . . . . .3 g
  Saturated Fat . . . . . . .1 g
Cholesterol . . . . .34 mg
Sodium . . . . .412 mg
Total Carbohydrate . . . .14 g
  Dietary Fiber . . . . . . .3 g
  Sugars . . . . .9 g
Protein . . . . .15 g

1 In a 2 1/2-quart or larger slow cooker, combine the onion, garlic, cabbage, green beans, carrots, and rice. Add the meat.

2 In a 4-cup measure or similar bowl, stir together the broth, tomato sauce, sugar, vinegar, thyme, mustard, and black pepper. Pour the mixture over the meat and vegetables.

3 Cover slow cooker, and cook for 1 hour on high. Stir meat and vegetables down into sauce, and cook an additional 8 to 8 1/2 hours on low.

EASY BEEF AND BLACK-BEAN CHILI

Here's one of those convenient slow-cooker meals that you can start in the morning and dish up for supper when you return from work.

1/2 *lb extra-lean ground beef*

2 *celery stalks, finely chopped*

1/4 *cup chopped green bell pepper, or*
1 4-oz can mild green chiles, drained

2 *Tbsp dehydrated minced onions*

3 *15-oz cans black beans, rinsed and drained*

1 *15-oz can low-sodium tomato sauce*

3 *beef bouillon cubes or*
1 Tbsp granules dissolved in
1/2 cup hot water

2 *tsp packed light or dark brown sugar*

1 1/2 *Tbsp mild to medium-hot chili powder*

1 1/2 *tsp ground allspice*

1/4 *tsp black pepper, or to taste*

1/4 *tsp salt, or to taste*

PREP TIME: 20 MINUTES

SERVINGS: 7

SERVING SIZE: 1 CUP

Exchanges
2 Starch
1 Vegetable
1 Lean Meat
1/2 Fat

Calories 278
  Calories from Fat 59
Total Fat . . . . .7 g
  Saturated Fat . . . . .2 g
Cholesterol . . . . .22 mg
Sodium . . . . .699 mg
Total Carbohydrate . . . .37 g
  Dietary Fiber . . . . . . .13 g
  Sugars . . . . .8 g
Protein . . . . .18 g

1 Put the ground beef in a 3-quart or larger slow cooker, breaking and crumbling it as finely as possible as it is added. Add the celery, green peppers (or green chiles), and onions. Mix the vegetables in well.

2 Stir in the black beans, tomato sauce, bouillon-water mixture, brown sugar, chili powder, allspice, black pepper, and salt until evenly incorporated.

3 Cover and turn to high setting. Cook at least 5 hours and up to 10 hours. Stir well. Taste and add more salt, if desired.

Mom's Ground Beef and Vegetable Soup

"This good, family-pleasing soup can be started in the morning and is ready to serve when you return home in the evening. Since the ground beef and carrots must be browned before being added to the slow cooker, you may want to prepare them the night before, then refrigerate them until assembling all the ingredients the next morning."

1/2 lb extra-lean ground beef

2 large carrots, sliced crosswise into thin slices

1 tsp Italian herb seasoning (or 1/2 tsp each dried oregano and basil leaves)

2 low-sodium beef bouillon cubes or granules dissolved in 1 1/2 cups hot water

3 cups vegetable juice, such as V8 or tomato juice

2 Tbsp dehydrated minced onions

2 large bay leaves

1 tsp sugar

1/4 to 1/2 tsp garlic salt, to taste

1/4 tsp black pepper

1/4 cup small soup pasta such as stars, tiny tubes, or small macaroni

1 14-oz package frozen (thawed) corn, red bell pepper, celery, and black bean medley or similar frozen vegetable combination

1 1/2 cups frozen (thawed) cut green beans

PREP TIME: 25 MINUTES

SERVINGS: 8

SERVING SIZE: 1 CUP

Exchanges
1/2 Starch
2 Vegetable
1 Lean Meat

Calories 165
    Calories from Fat 33
Total Fat . . . . .4 g
    Saturated Fat . . . . .1 g
Cholesterol . . . . .18 mg
Sodium . . . . .330 mg
Total Carbohydrate . . . .20 g
    Dietary Fiber . . . . .5 g
    Sugars . . . . .8 g
Protein . . . . .10 g

1 Combine the beef, carrots, and Italian herb seasoning in a 12-inch nonstick skillet over medium-high heat. Cook, stirring to break up the beef, until it is just cooked through, about 6 minutes.

2 Put the cooked beef mixture in a 3-quart or larger slow cooker. Stir in the water-bouillon mixture, vegetable juice, onions, bay leaves, sugar, 1/4 teaspoon garlic salt, pepper, and pasta. Stir in the frozen vegetable medley and green beans. (The liquid may not cover all the vegetables at this point.)

3 Cover the cooker, and turn on the high setting for at least 30 and preferably 45 minutes. Turn to the low setting and cook for at least 5 hours and up to 10 hours. Thin the soup with a little hot water before serving, if desired. Taste and add more garlic salt, if desired.

4 Discard the bay leaves as the soup is served.

SLOPPY JOE STEW

Traditionally, this savory ground beef mixture is used for sandwiches, but we like to serve our super-convenient slow-cooker version as a stew over rice. You could simply spoon the mixture onto buns (preferably whole-grain) instead.

3/4 lb extra-lean ground beef round

1 large onion, finely chopped

2 1/2 cups thinly sliced green cabbage

2 celery stalks, finely chopped

3/4 tsp ground allspice

2 reduced-sodium or regular beef bouillon cubes or 2 tsp beef bouillon granules, dissolved in 1/4 cup hot water

2 15-oz cans low-sodium or regular tomato sauce

1 1/2 Tbsp Worcestershire sauce

1 Tbsp Splenda

1/4 tsp black pepper, or to taste

Salt to taste (optional)

3 cups hot cooked long-grain brown or white rice

PREP TIME: 20 MINUTES

SERVINGS: 6

SERVING SIZE: 1 CUP STEW, PLUS 1/2 CUP RICE

Exchanges
2 Starch
2 Vegetable
2 Lean Meat

Calories 268
   Calories from Fat 36
Total Fat . . . . .4 g
   Saturated Fat . . . . .1 g
Cholesterol . . . . .30 mg
Sodium . . . . .274 mg
Total Carbohydrate . . . .41 g
   Dietary Fiber . . . . .6 g
   Sugars . . . . .4 g
Protein . . . . .17 g

1 Combine the ground beef, onion, cabbage, celery, and allspice in a 12-inch nonstick skillet over medium-high heat. Cook, stirring to break up the beef, until it is just cooked through, about 6 minutes.

2 Put the cooked beef mixture in a 3-quart or larger slow cooker. Add the bouillon-water mixture, tomato sauce, Worcestershire sauce, Splenda, black pepper, and salt, if desired, and stir well.

3 Cover and cook on the high setting for 4 or 5 hours or on the low setting for 9 or 10 hours.

4 Stir well. Spoon over rice, and serve.

NAVY BEAN SOUP WITH HAM

"This is a good, hearty, economical, and convenient soup! We like to put the beans in the slow cooker in the evening so they can cook during the night. Then, we start the soup the next morning before leaving for the day. There's a fuss-free supper waiting when we return hours later. (We usually add a salad to round out the meal.)"

1 lb package dried navy beans, rinsed and drained

4 beef bouillon cubes dissolved in 3 cups hot water

1 medium smoked pork hock (about 1/2 lb)

2 medium carrots, diced

1 medium onion, chopped

1 large celery stalk, diced

1 medium red bell pepper, diced

1/3 cup ketchup

1 Tbsp prepared mustard

1 Tbsp clover honey or other mild honey

2 large bay leaves

1/2 tsp ground allspice

1 1/4 cups coarsely diced lean smoked ham

Salt and black pepper to taste (optional)

PREP TIME: 20 MINUTES

SERVINGS: 9

SERVING SIZE: 1 CUP

Exchanges
2 1/2 Starch
1 Lean Meat
1 Vegetable

Calories 272
   Calories from Fat 41
Total Fat . . . . .5 g
   Saturated Fat . . . . .1 g
Cholesterol . . . . .18 mg
Sodium . . . . .946 mg
Total Carbohydrate . . . .43 g
   Dietary Fiber . . . . .9 g
   Sugars . . . . .9 g
Protein . . . . .17 g

1 In a 3-quart or larger slow cooker, combine the beans with enough hot water to cover them by at least 4 1/2 inches. Cook on the high setting for at least 5 hours and up to 12 hours. Turn out the beans into a colander; rinse and drain them well under hot water.

2 Immediately return the beans to the slow cooker, along with the water-bouillon cube mixture. (Keep the cooker on high.) Add the pork hock, carrot, onion, celery, bell pepper, ketchup, mustard, honey, bay leaves, and allspice; stir to mix. Cover and cook at least 3 hours and up to 10 hours, until the vegetables and beans are very tender.

3 Discard the pork hock and bay leaves from the pot. Stir the ham into the soup. Continue cooking until piping hot. Add salt and pepper to taste, if desired.

EASY LENTIL-VEGETABLE SOUP

Here's one of those slow-cooker recipes that can be started in the morning before going to work and served for supper when you return. The soup is tastier and more full-bodied when it includes a little lean ham or Canadian bacon, but in a pinch these can be omitted. In this case, the flavor will be very mild, and you may need to add more salt and pepper.

2 cups uncooked brown or green
    lentils, rinsed and drained

3 beef bouillon cubes or 1 Tbsp granules
    dissolved in 6 1/2 cups very hot water

1 medium smoked pork hock
    (about 1/2 lb)

1 medium onion, chopped

1 large celery stalk, diced

1 medium carrot, diced

1 1/2 cups frozen (thawed) succotash

1 tsp dried thyme leaves

1/2 tsp ground allspice

1/4 tsp black pepper

1 cup lean, well-trimmed, diced smoked
    ham or Canadian bacon (optional)

Salt to taste

PREP TIME: 20 MINUTES

SERVINGS: 10

SERVING SIZE: 1 CUP

Exchanges
2 Starch
1 Very Lean Meat

Calories 179
   Calories from Fat 30
Total Fat . . . . .3 g
   Saturated Fat . . . . .1 g
Cholesterol . . . . .7 mg
Sodium . . . . .445 mg
Total Carbohydrate . . . .27 g
   Dietary Fiber . . . . .9 g
   Sugars . . . . .4 g
Protein . . . . .12 g

1 In a 3-quart or larger slow cooker, combine the lentils, bouillon-water mixture, pork hock, onion, celery, carrot, succotash, thyme, allspice, and pepper. Cover and set cooker to high. Cook at least 5 and up to 9 hours, until the lentils are very tender and falling apart.

2 Discard the pork hock from the pot. Add the ham or Canadian bacon, if desired, stirring well. Heat until piping hot. Add salt and more pepper to taste. (The soup will thicken upon standing. Thin it with hot water to the desired consistency before serving.)

SAUSAGE, BEAN, AND VEGETABLE SOUP

"Good flavor and ease of preparation make this homey, stick-to-the-ribs soup a winner. It's important to use low-sodium beef broth or granules in this recipe as the tomato juice is rather salty."

1 10-oz package frozen (thawed) mixed vegetables (such as corn, limas, peas, carrots, and green beans)

1/4 cup uncooked green or brown lentils

3 Tbsp dehydrated minced onions

1 large bay leaf

1/2 tsp dried thyme leaves

1/4 tsp black pepper

3 cups tomato juice

2 cups low-sodium beef broth or 2 tsp low-sodium beef bouillon granules dissolved in 2 cups hot water

1 14-oz can great northern beans, rinsed and drained

1 12-oz lean turkey kielbasa sausage, cut crosswise into 1/4-inch slices

4 1/2 cups coarsely chopped green cabbage

1/4 tsp salt, or to taste (optional)

PREP TIME: 20 MINUTES

SERVINGS: 10

SERVING SIZE: 1 CUP

Exchanges
1 Starch
1 Lean Meat
1 Vegetable

Calories 159
   Calories from Fat 33
Total Fat . . . . .4 g
   Saturated Fat . . . . .1 g
Cholesterol . . . . .19 mg
Sodium . . . . .791 mg
Total Carbohydrate . . . .23 g
   Dietary Fiber . . . . .5 g
   Sugars . . . . .7 g
Protein . . . . .11 g

1 In a 3-quart or larger slow cooker, thoroughly stir together the vegetables, lentils, onions, bay leaf, thyme, pepper, tomato juice, and broth (or bouillon-water mixture). Top with the beans, then the sausage and the cabbage; do not stir these into the liquid. (The liquid will not cover the cabbage at this point.)

2 Cover the cooker and turn on the high setting for at least 30 and preferably 45 minutes. Turn to the low setting and cook for at least 6 hours and up to 9 hours, if preferred. If the cabbage is not tender, stir it into the liquid, raise the heat to high, and cook 15 minutes longer. If desired, thin the soup with a little hot water before serving. Taste and add the salt, if desired.

3 Discard the bay leaf as the soup is served.

BLACK-EYED PEA, COLLARDS, AND HAM STEAK DINNER

Enjoy a taste of the South in this healthful slow-cooker dinner. Be sure to use no-sodium chicken bouillon granules, as pork hocks are often rather salty.

1 10-oz package frozen black-eyed peas, rinsed and well drained

2 tsp no-sodium chicken bouillon granules dissolved in 1 1/2 cups very hot water

1 small smoked pork hock (about 1/3 lb), trimmed of excess fat

1 medium onion, chopped

2 large celery ribs, chopped

1/2 tsp dried thyme leaves

1/4 tsp crushed hot red pepper flakes

12 to 14 oz fresh collard greens (untrimmed), stems removed

12 oz boneless, reduced-fat, lower-sodium, fully cooked ham steaks, trimmed of excess fat and cut into 3/4-inch cubes

Salt and black pepper to taste

PREP TIME: 25 MINUTES

SERVINGS: 5

SERVING SIZE: 1 1/2 CUPS

Exchanges
1 Starch
1 Vegetable
2 Lean Meat

Calories 234
   Calories from Fat 54
Total Fat . . . . .6 g
   Saturated Fat . . . . .2 g
Cholesterol . . . . .39 mg
Sodium . . . . .699 mg
Total Carbohydrate . . . .23 g
   Dietary Fiber . . . . .6 g
   Sugars . . . . .2 g
Protein . . . . .22 g

1 In a 3-quart or larger slow cooker, combine the peas, hot water-bouillon mixture, pork hock, onion, celery, thyme, and red pepper flakes. Turn the cooker to the low setting.

2 Bring a tea kettle of water to a boil. Meanwhile, rinse the greens in a colander under running water. Pull the leafy parts from the ribs, discarding any coarse ribs and tearing the leaves in 2- to 3-inch pieces. Rinse the leaves again. Put them in a large bowl of water, swishing them around. Let stand so any loosened grit can sink to the bottom. Lift out the leaves; return them to the colander. Slowly pour the boiling water all over the greens until they are wilted. Let them drain well.

3 Add the greens to the pot, stirring them down into the liquid. Cook 6 to 8 hours, until the peas and collards are tender. Add the ham steak pieces. Set cooker on high, and heat just until piping hot. Discard the pork hock from the pot. Add salt and pepper to taste, if desired.

PINTO BEAN, CORN, AND BELL PEPPER POT

" Pinto beans have a mild, yet distinctive flavor that goes well with corn and bell peppers. We like to dress up this good, stick-to-the-ribs soup with tortilla chips, grated cheese, salsa, and cilantro or green onions, although it can be served plain. "

1 lb pinto beans, rinsed and drained

1 medium smoked pork hock (about 1/2 lb)

1 14- to 16-oz package frozen (thawed) bell pepper and onion stir-fry medley

1 10-oz package frozen (thawed) succotash

3 cups fat-free low-sodium or regular chicken broth

1 1/2 tsp mild to hot chili powder

1/4 tsp caraway seeds or cumin seeds

1/2 tsp salt

1/4 tsp black pepper, or to taste

Pinch dried hot red pepper flakes (optional)

GARNISHES

2 cups coarsely broken baked tortilla chips

1 cup (4 oz) shredded, reduced-fat sharp cheddar cheese

1/2 cup chunky salsa or taco sauce

1/4 cup chopped cilantro or green onions (optional)

PREP TIME: 25 MINUTES

SERVINGS: 9

SERVING SIZE: 1 CUP

Exchanges
3 Starch
1 Lean Meat
1/2 Fat

Calories 306
    Calories from Fat 62
Total Fat . . . . .7 g
    Saturated Fat . . . . . . .3 g
Cholesterol . . . . .17 mg
Sodium . . . . .703 mg
Total Carbohydrate . . . .46 g
    Dietary Fiber . . . . . . .12 g
    Sugars . . . . .6 g
Protein . . . . .18 g

1 In a 3-quart or larger slow cooker, combine the beans with enough hot water to cover them by at least 4 1/2 inches. Cook on high for at least 5 hours and up to 12 hours. Turn out the beans into a colander; rinse under hot water and drain them well.

2 Place the pork hock, pepper-onion mixture, and succotash in the slow cooker.

3 Add the broth, chili powder, caraway seed, salt, pepper, and hot pepper flakes (if using), stirring to mix.

4 Return the beans to the slow cooker. (A 3-quart cooker will be full and the beans will not be covered with liquid at this point.) Turn the setting to high. Cover and cook at least 5 hours and up to 8 hours, until the vegetables and beans are very tender and falling apart.

5 Discard the pork hock from the pot. To serve, ladle the soup into large soup plates. Top each serving with some tortilla chips, cheese, salsa, and cilantro (or green onions). Serve immediately.

BAVARIAN BEEF STEW

The slow cooker creates a perfect blend of flavors in this unusual stew.

 1 lb stew beef, trimmed of
    fat, cubed
 1 15-oz can low-sodium or
    regular tomato sauce
 1 cup canned sauerkraut
 1 large onion, chopped
15 baby carrots
 2 celery stalks
 1 1/2 Tbsp sugar
 1 1/2 tsp caraway seeds
 1/8 tsp black pepper
 5 oz (about 1 1/2 cups) eggless
    egg noodles

1 In a 2-quart or larger slow cooker, combine the
beef, tomato sauce, sauerkraut, onion, carrots,
celery, sugar, caraway seeds, and pepper.

2 Cover and cook on high setting 1 hour. Reduce
heat, and cook on low setting for 4 or 5 hours.

3 Cook the noodles according to package directions.
Serve the beef and vegetables over noodles.

PREP TIME: 20 MINUTES

SERVINGS: 5

SERVING SIZE: 1 CUP, PLUS
    1 OZ NOODLES

Exchanges
1 1/2 Starch
2 Lean Meat
3 Vegetable

Calories 313
    Calories from Fat 51
Total Fat . . . . .6 g
    Saturated Fat . . . . .2 g
Cholesterol . . . . .54 mg
Sodium . . . . .433 mg
Total Carbohydrate . . . .39 g
    Dietary Fiber . . . . .6 g
    Sugars . . . . .15 g
Protein . . . . .26 g

MAIN DISH SALADS

CHICKEN-BROCCOLI-PASTA SALAD

" If you like, you can mix broccoli and cauliflower in this chunky chicken salad. "

3/4 cup uncooked penne pasta

1/2 cup reduced-fat mayonnaise

1/4 cup nonfat buttermilk

1 tsp poultry seasoning

1/4 tsp salt, or to taste (optional)

3 1/2 cups cooked chicken breast, cut into bite-sized pieces

5 cups small broccoli florets

1 cup chopped red cabbage

1/2 cup chopped pecans

1 Cook the pasta according to package directions. Cool under running water.

2 While pasta is cooking, in a large bowl whisk together the mayonnaise, buttermilk, poultry seasoning, and salt, if desired. Stir in the chicken, broccoli, cabbage, nuts, and pasta.

3 Serve immediately, or refrigerate several hours or overnight.

PREP TIME: 20 MINUTES

SERVINGS: 9

SERVING SIZE: 1 CUP

Exchanges
1/2 Starch
3 Lean Meat
2 Fat

Calories 222
   Calories from Fat . . .100
Total Fat . . . . .11 g
   Saturated Fat . . . . .1 g
Cholesterol . . . . .51 mg
Sodium . . . . .167 mg
Total Carbohydrate . . . .10 g
   Dietary Fiber . . . . .2 g
   Sugars . . . . .2 g
Protein . . . . .20 g

BROCCOLI, HAM, AND CHEESE SALAD

"This salad gets rave reviews—for the tangy flavor and interesting combination of ingredients. For best results, use mayonnaise with 5 grams of fat per tablespoon."

1/4 cup reduced-fat mayonnaise

2 Tbsp nonfat buttermilk

1 Tbsp cider vinegar

2 tsp granulated sugar

5 cups small broccoli florets

6 oz fully cooked, low-fat ham, diced (about 1 1/2 cups)

1 cup grated or shredded reduced-fat cheddar cheese

1 cup cooked penne or similar pasta

1/4 cup chopped red onion

PREP TIME: 20 MINUTES

SERVINGS: 7

SERVING SIZE:
    1 GENEROUS CUP

Exchanges
1/2 Starch
1 Vegetable
4 Lean Meat
1/2 Fat

Calories 149
    Calories from Fat 68
Total Fat . . . . .8 g
    Saturated Fat . . . . .3 g
Cholesterol . . . . .26 mg
Sodium . . . . .520 mg
Total Carbohydrate . . . .11 g
    Dietary Fiber . . . . .2 g
    Sugars . . . . .4 g
Protein . . . . .33 g

1 Place the mayonnaise in a large bowl. Slowly whisk in the buttermilk until well combined. Add the vinegar and sugar, and whisk until well combined.

2 Add the broccoli, ham, cheese, pasta, and onion, and toss with the dressing. Serve at once, or refrigerate several hours before serving. The salad can be kept in the refrigerator for 2 or 3 days. Stir before serving.

CURRIED CHICKEN SALAD

This flavorful chicken salad is a good dish to make when you have leftover cooked basmati rice. If you like, you can make the recipe with regular cooked white rice as well.

1/4 cup reduced-fat mayonnaise

1/4 cup nonfat sour cream

1 1/2 tsp mild curry powder, or to taste

1/4 tsp salt, or to taste (optional)

1/8 tsp ground white pepper

3 or 4 drops hot pepper sauce

1 8-oz can crushed juice-packed pineapple, drained

1 cup cooked basmati rice, chilled

3/4 lb cooked boneless, skinless chicken breast

1 8-oz can water chestnuts, well drained

1 celery stalk, thinly sliced

1/3 cup chopped chives or sliced green onion tops

Iceberg or other lettuce leaves

PREP TIME: 17 MINUTES

SERVINGS: 4

SERVING SIZE: 1 CUP, PLUS LETTUCE

Exchanges
1 Starch
1/2 Fruit
2 Vegetable
3 Very Lean Meat
1 1/2 Fat

Calories 321
    Calories from Fat 75
Total Fat . . . . .8 g
    Saturated Fat . . . . . . .2 g
Cholesterol . . . . .78 mg
Sodium . . . . .221 mg
Total Carbohydrate . . . .31 g
    Dietary Fiber . . . . . . .3 g
    Sugars . . . . .11 g
Protein . . . . .29 g

1 In a large bowl, combine the mayonnaise and sour cream. Whisk to combine. Whisk in the curry powder, salt and pepper, and hot pepper sauce; stir to mix well. Stir in the pineapple and rice.

2 Cut the chicken into small bite-sized pieces. Stir into the salad mixture. Stir in the water chestnuts, celery, and chives (or onion tops).

3 Serve at once mounded on lettuce leaves. Or cover and refrigerate for several hours.

Pasta-Chicken Salad with Lemon Vinaigrette

" This salad is light and refreshing and makes a tempting hot-weather meal. "

1 lb boneless, skinless chicken breast
   halves, cut in thirds lengthwise

1/2 cup fat-free low-sodium or regular
   chicken broth

3/4 cup orzo (rice-shaped pasta) or other
   very small pasta shape

Scant 1/3 cup fresh lemon juice, or to taste

2 1/2 Tbsp olive oil

1/2 tsp salt

1/4 tsp black pepper

3 medium celery stalks, chopped

1 cup chopped red bell pepper

1 cup chopped cauliflower florets

1 cup chopped parsley leaves

3 Tbsp chopped fresh chives or finely
   chopped green onion

Tomato wedges and lettuce leaves for
   garnish

PREP TIME: 25 MINUTES

SERVINGS: 4

SERVING SIZE: 1 1/2 CUPS,
   PLUS TOMATO WEDGES
   AND LETTUCE LEAVES

Exchanges
1 1/2 Starch
2 Vegetable
3 Very Lean Meat
2 Fat

Calories	.365
Calories from Fat	.103
Total Fat	.11 g
Saturated Fat	.3 g
Cholesterol	.68 mg
Sodium	.474 mg
Total Carbohydrate	.34 g
Dietary Fiber	.4 g
Sugars	.5 g
Protein	.32 g

1 In a large saucepan over medium-high heat, combine the chicken pieces and broth. Simmer the chicken until just cooked through, about 6 to 9 minutes. Using a fork, remove the chicken from the pan and set aside to cool.

2 Add 2 1/2 cups water to the broth in the saucepan and bring to a boil over high heat. Add the orzo and boil about 5 minutes, or until the pasta is just barely tender. Turn the orzo out into a colander; rinse lightly under cold water. Drain well.

3 Stir together a scant 1/3 cup lemon juice, oil, salt, pepper, celery, bell pepper, cauliflower, parsley, and chives in a large, non-reactive bowl.

4 When the chicken is cool enough to handle, cut it into bite-sized pieces. Stir the chicken meat into the lemon vinaigrette.

5 Stir the drained orzo into the vinaigrette. Toss until well blended. Taste and add more lemon juice and salt and pepper, if desired. Serve the salad immediately, or if preferred, chill, and then serve. Serve garnished with lettuce leaves and tomato wedges.

MIDDLE-EASTERN-STYLE TURKEY SALAD

Here's a nice change from classic chicken salad. We've made it with cooked turkey breast to cut the fat and calories, but you can easily substitute cooked chicken breast. The dish tastes best when made with fresh mint.

1 cup dry bulgur wheat

1 1/2 cups boiling water

2 1/2 to 3 Tbsp lemon juice

2 Tbsp olive oil

1 1/2 tsp minced garlic

1 tsp salt, or to taste (optional)

2 to 3 drops hot pepper sauce (optional)

3 cups small, bite-sized pieces cooked turkey breast meat

1/4 cup thinly sliced green onion tops

1/2 cup chopped fresh parsley leaves

3 Tbsp fresh mint leaves or 2 tsp dried mint leaves

1 large cucumber, peeled, seeded, and diced

PREP TIME: 25 MINUTES

SERVINGS: 5

SERVING SIZE: 1 CUP

Exchanges
1 1/2 Starch
1 Vegetable
3 Very Lean Meat
1/2 Fat

Calories 277
    Calories from Fat 53
Total Fat . . . . .6 g
    Saturated Fat . . . . .1 g
Cholesterol . . . . .68 mg
Sodium . . . . .58 mg
Total Carbohydrate . . . .27 g
    Dietary Fiber . . . . .7 g
    Sugars . . . . .3 g
Protein . . . . .30 g

1 In a large bowl, combine the bulgur and boiling water. Cover and let stand 15 to 20 minutes, until the bulgur has softened and most of the water has been absorbed. Drain in a sieve. Return the bulgur to the bowl.

2 Add the lemon juice, oil, garlic, salt, if desired, and hot pepper sauce, if desired. Stir to mix well.

3 Stir in the turkey, onion, parsley, mint, and cucumber.

4 Serve at once, or cover and refrigerate several hours. Stir before serving.

To Your Health
Turkey-Vegetable Salad

Our lightened-up turkey salad is succulent and tasty. One secret is in using poached rather than roasted white turkey meat; the gentle cooking in seasoned broth keeps the meat very juicy and infuses it with flavor. Another secret is in relying on reduced-fat mayonnaise and jazzing it up with some savory herbs. We like to serve the salad on a bed of lettuce garnished with tomato wedges and cucumber slices.

1 1/2 lb boneless, skinless turkey breast meat

2 cups fat-free low-sodium or regular chicken broth

1 tsp dried marjoram leaves or tarragon leaves

1/2 cup reduced-fat mayonnaise

2 Tbsp chopped fresh chives or finely chopped green onion

1 Tbsp Dijon-style mustard

1 Tbsp apple cider vinegar

2 1/2 cups chopped celery

2 cups finely chopped cauliflower florets

1 cup frozen green peas, thawed

1/4 tsp salt (optional)

Tomato wedges, cucumber slices, and lettuce leaves for garnish

PREP TIME: 20 MINUTES

SERVINGS: 4

SERVING SIZE: 1 1/2 CUPS

Exchanges
3 Very Lean Meat
2 Vegetable
1 Fat

Calories 190
    Calories from Fat 54
Total Fat . . . . .6 g
    Saturated Fat . . . . . . .1 g
Cholesterol . . . . .58 mg
Sodium . . . . .303 mg
Total Carbohydrate . . . .10 g
    Dietary Fiber . . . . .3 g
    Sugars . . . . .4 g
Protein . . . . .24 g

1 Cut the turkey meat into 4 or 5 equal pieces.

2 In a 2- to 3-quart saucepan over medium-high heat, combine the turkey pieces, broth, and marjoram (or tarragon). Adjust the heat so the broth simmers; cook, covered, until the turkey is just cooked through when cut into and checked in the thickest part, 12 to 16 minutes. Remove from the heat; let the turkey stand in the broth until cool enough to handle.

3 Combine the mayonnaise, chives (or onion), mustard, and vinegar in a large non-reactive bowl; stir well. Stir in the celery, cauliflower, and peas until evenly incorporated.

4 When the turkey is cooled, cut it into bite-sized chunks; you should have about 4 cups of meat. Stir the turkey and 2 tablespoons of the cooking broth into the mayonnaise-vegetable mixture. Toss until very well blended. Taste and add salt, if desired.

5 Cover and refrigerate at least 30 minutes and up to 2 days. Serve the salad on lettuce leaves, garnished with tomato wedges and cucumber slices.

Handy Tip

If the market where you shop sells only bone-in turkey breast halves, either ask the butcher to remove the skin and cut the meat from the bone for you, or do this yourself at home. You'll need about a 2 1/2- to 2 3/4-pound bone-in breast half to yield the necessary 1 1/2 pounds of meat.

Spicy Shrimp, Pasta, and Vegetable Salad

" We love the fresh, tangy taste of this easy salad. *"*

PASTA

   1 1/2 cups uncooked penne, or similar pasta

DRESSING

   1/2 cup low-sodium or regular tomato sauce

   1/3 cup reduced-fat mayonnaise

   1 Tbsp cider vinegar

   2 tsp granulated sugar

   1/2 tsp chili powder

   1/2 tsp minced garlic

   1/4 tsp salt (optional)

   1/8 tsp black pepper, or to taste

SHRIMP AND VEGETABLES

   1 lb ready-to-serve medium shrimp

   1 1/2 cups small cauliflower florets, blanched
      if desired

   1/2 large red or yellow bell pepper, diced

   1 large celery stalk, sliced

   2 Tbsp chopped red onion

   Iceberg or other lettuce leaves

   Chopped parsley for garnish (optional)

PREP TIME: 20 MINUTES

SERVINGS: 8

SERVING SIZE: 1 CUP,
   PLUS LETTUCE

Exchanges
1 Starch
1 Vegetable
1 Very Lean Meat
1/2 Fat

Calories 168
   Calories from Fat 39
Total Fat . . . . .4 g
   Saturated Fat . . . . .1 g
Cholesterol . . . . .113 mg
Sodium . . . . .227 mg
Total Carbohydrate . . . .17 g
   Dietary Fiber . . . . .2 g
   Sugars . . . . .4 g
Protein . . . . .15 g

1 Cook the pasta according to package directions. Cool under cold running water. Drain well in a colander, and set aside.

2 Meanwhile, in a large bowl, combine the tomato sauce, mayonnaise, vinegar, sugar, chili powder, garlic, salt, if desired, and black pepper. Whisk to mix well.

3 Add the shrimp to the bowl, along with the reserved pasta, cauliflower, bell pepper, celery, and onion. Stir to coat with dressing. Serve immediately, or cover and refrigerate several hours until flavors are well blended.

4 To serve, line a large serving platter with lettuce leaves, and mound the salad on top. Or serve individual portions on lettuce leaves. Garnish with parsley, if desired.

PANZANELLA SHRIMP SALAD

This Mediterranean salad makes an appealing summer lunch or supper entree. To save time, we use frozen shrimp, but fresh cooked and peeled ones could be used as well.

1 1/2 cups day-old French or Italian
    bread cubes (1/2-inch)

3 1/2 Tbsp fresh lemon juice

2 1/2 Tbsp olive oil, preferably extra-virgin

3 Tbsp finely chopped green onion or
    chopped fresh chives

1/2 tsp dry mustard

1/2 tsp celery salt

1/4 tsp black pepper

1 lb frozen (thawed) peeled and cooked
    medium shrimp

1 cup chopped cauliflower florets

1 cup coarsely chopped celery

1 cup diced red, yellow, or green bell pepper,
    or a combination

1 cup coarsely diced zucchini

1/4 cup pitted and sliced Nicoise or Kalamata
    black olives

1 Tbsp chopped fresh basil or marjoram
    leaves, or 1 tsp dried basil leaves

1 1/2 cups coarsely diced, flavorful, fully ripe
    tomatoes

Crisp lettuce leaves for garnish

PREP TIME: 25 MINUTES

SERVINGS: 5

SERVING SIZE: 1 1/2 CUPS,
PLUS CRISP LETTUCE
LEAVES FOR GARNISH

Exchanges
1/2 Starch
1 Vegetable
2 Very Lean Meat
1 1/2 Fat

Calories 217
   Calories from Fat 78
Total Fat . . . . .9 g
   Saturated Fat . . . . .1 g
Cholesterol . . . . .176 mg
Sodium . . . . .482 mg
Total Carbohydrate . . . .14 g
   Dietary Fiber . . . . .3 g
   Sugars . . . . .4 g
Protein . . . . .22 g

1 Preheat the oven to 400 degrees. Spread the bread in a small baking pan. Toast, stirring several times, until the cubes are browned and crispy, about 6 to 9 minutes. Set aside to cool.

2 In a medium non-reactive bowl, stir together the lemon juice, oil, green onion (or chives), mustard, celery salt, and pepper. Stir in the shrimp, and set aside while the vegetables are prepared.

3 In a large bowl, stir together the cauliflower, celery, bell pepper, zucchini, olives, and basil. Add the dressing and shrimp to the vegetables, stirring well.

4 Just before serving, add the tomatoes and toasted bread cubes, tossing lightly to mix. Serve the salad on lettuce leaves.

Handy Tip

If you wish, the vegetables, shrimp, and dressing can be readied up to 24 hours ahead and refrigerated. Then, the bread cubes and tomatoes can be tossed in at the last minute.

MEDITERRANEAN SALMON SALAD

Here's a nice way to dress up canned salmon. We love the pleasing mix of tastes and textures. If you prefer, you can use a simple homemade oil and vinegar dressing.

8 cups torn romaine lettuce

1 15-oz can chickpeas, rinsed
and drained

1 1/2 cups sliced white mushrooms

16 grape tomatoes

1/2 cup grated feta cheese

1/4 cup sliced green onion tops

2 6-oz cans skinless, boneless pink salmon,
drained and flaked

1/2 cup bottled Greek-style oil and vinegar
dressing

1 In a large salad bowl, toss together lettuce, chickpeas, mushrooms, tomatoes, feta cheese, and onions. Mix in salmon.

2 Add salad dressing and toss. Serve at once.

PREP TIME: 15 MINUTES

SERVINGS: 5

SERVING SIZE:
    2 GENEROUS CUPS

Exchanges
1 Starch
2 Vegetable
2 Lean Meat

Calories 245
    Calories from Fat 71
Total Fat . . . . .8 g
    Saturated Fat . . . . .2 g
Cholesterol . . . . .54 mg
Sodium . . . . .1574 mg
Total Carbohydrate . . . .25 g
    Dietary Fiber . . . . . . .5 g
    Sugars . . . . .9 g
Protein . . . . .18 g

CHUNKY GREEK-STYLE SALAD WITH TUNA

Here's a salad with lots of crunch—and lots of flavor.

3 *Tbsp olive oil*
1/2 *Tbsp red wine vinegar*
1/2 *tsp dried thyme leaves*
1/2 *tsp dried basil leaves*
1/2 *cup crumbled reduced-fat feta cheese*
6 *cups mixed salad greens*
5 *oil-cured pitted Greek olives, chopped*
1 *small cucumber, peeled and cubed*
2 *Tbsp sliced green onion*
1 *medium tomato, cubed*
1 *6-oz can water-packed albacore tuna, well drained*
1 *cup seasoned croutons*

1 In a large bowl, combine oil, vinegar, thyme, and basil. Stir to mix well.

2 Stir in the cheese. Add the greens, olives, cucumber, onion, and tomato. Toss to coat with dressing.

3 Add tuna and croutons; toss. Serve immediately.

PREP TIME: 9 MINUTES

SERVINGS: 5 1/3

SERVING SIZE: 1 1/2 CUPS

Exchanges
2 Vegetable
1 1/2 Lean Meat
1 Fat

Calories	191
Calories from Fat	99
Total Fat	11 g
Saturated Fat	2 g
Cholesterol	24 mg
Sodium	428 mg
Total Carbohydrate	10 g
Dietary Fiber	2 g
Sugars	2 g
Protein	13 g

Salmon, Potato, and Green Bean Salad

Here's a tasty combination of ingredients that adds up to a hearty and satisfying salad.

3 cups 1/2-inch red-skin potato cubes

3 cups petite frozen green bean pieces

1/4 cup reduced-fat mayonnaise

1/4 cup nonfat sour cream

1 Tbsp Dijon-style mustard

1 Tbsp balsamic vinegar

1/4 cup chopped red onion

1 red bell pepper, seeded and diced

1 tsp dried basil leaves

1 14 3/4-oz can skinless, boneless pink salmon, drained, skin and bones removed

3 cups romaine or other lettuce leaves

PREP TIME: 14 MINUTES

SERVINGS: 9

SERVING SIZE: 1 CUP, PLUS LETTUCE

Exchanges
1 1/2 Starch
1 Vegetable
1 Lean Meat
1/2 Fat

Calories 154
    Calories from Fat 47
Total Fat . . . . .5 g
    Saturated Fat . . . . .0 g
Cholesterol . . . . .29 mg
Sodium . . . . .368 mg
Total Carbohydrate . . . .15 g
    Dietary Fiber . . . . .3 g
    Sugars . . . . .4 g
Protein . . . . .12 g

1 Combine the potatoes and green beans in a large pot. Cover with water, bring to a boil, and cook 6 to 8 minutes or until the potatoes are tender. Transfer to a colander, cool under running water, and drain.

2 Meanwhile, in a large bowl, whisk together the mayonnaise, sour cream, mustard, and vinegar. Stir in the onion, pepper, and basil. Stir in cooked green beans and potatoes. Flake salmon in a medium bowl, and then carefully fold into the salad mixture.

3 Arrange lettuce leaves on plates. Mound salad over lettuce.

TUNA-PASTA SALAD

A light vinaigrette dressing gives this easy, colorful salad a zesty flavor. Though the homemade dressing is simple to make, to save time, you could use a half-cup of bottled low-fat oil and vinegar dressing instead.

5 oz (about 1 1/2 cups) ziti or other medium tube-shaped pasta, cooked according to package directions

3 medium celery stalks, diced moderately fine

2 medium carrots, diced moderately fine

1 cup small cauliflower florets

1 cup grape tomatoes

2 Tbsp chopped fresh chives or finely chopped green onion (optional)

2 6-oz cans water-packed, solid white albacore tuna, well drained

DRESSING

1/3 cup apple cider vinegar, or to taste

2 1/2 Tbsp olive oil

3/4 tsp celery salt

1/4 tsp black pepper

PREP TIME: 15 MINUTES

SERVINGS: 5

SERVING SIZE: 2 CUPS

Exchanges
2 Starch
2 Vegetable
2 Very Lean Meat
1 Fat

Calories 294
    Calories from Fat 66
Total Fat . . . . .8 g
    Saturated Fat . . . . .2 g
Cholesterol . . . . .18 mg
Sodium . . . . .460 mg
Total Carbohydrate . . . .36 g
    Dietary Fiber . . . . .4 g
    Sugars . . . . .8 g
Protein . . . . .22 g

1 In a very large non-reactive bowl stir together the cooled pasta, celery, carrots, cauliflower, tomatoes, and chives (or green onion), if using. Add the tuna, being careful not to break it up too much.

2 In a small non-reactive bowl, stir together the vinegar, oil, celery salt, and pepper until well blended. Pour the dressing over the salad, tossing until evenly incorporated.

GREEK-STYLE STEAK SALAD

Strips of steak turn Greek salad into lunch or dinner. To round out the meal, serve with whole-wheat rolls.

1/2 lb sirloin steak, trimmed of all fat
    Salt and pepper to taste (optional)
1/4 cup canola oil
  1 Tbsp red wine vinegar
1/2 tsp dried thyme leaves
1/2 tsp dried basil leaves
1/2 cup crumbled fat-free feta cheese
  8 cups mixed salad greens
 10 Greek olives, pitted and sliced
1 1/2 cups cucumber, peeled, seeded, and sliced
1/4 cup chopped red onion
1 3/4 cup cubed tomato
  6 whole-wheat rolls (optional)

1 Sprinkle the steak with salt and pepper. Broil or grill according to desired degree of doneness.

2 Meanwhile, in a large bowl, combine the oil, vinegar, thyme, and basil. Stir to mix well. Stir in the cheese. Add the greens, olives, cucumber, onion, and tomato. Toss to coat with dressing.

3 Allow steak to cool slightly. Cut into 3/4-inch pieces. Toss with salad. Serve immediately with whole-wheat rolls, if desired.

PREP TIME: 15 MINUTES

SERVINGS: 6

SERVING SIZE: 1 1/2 CUPS

Exchanges
1 1/2 Vegetable
1 Medium-Fat Meat
2 Fat

Calories 194
    Calories from Fat . . .126
Total Fat . . . . .14 g
    Saturated Fat . . . . .2 g
Cholesterol . . . . .18 mg
Sodium . . . . .285 mg
Total Carbohydrate . . . . .7 g
    Dietary Fiber . . . . .2 g
    Sugars . . . . .3 g
Protein . . . . .10 g

HEARTY SANDWICHES AND WRAPS

Barbecued Chicken Sandwiches

" These sandwiches feature bite-sized pieces of chicken in a tangy barbecue sauce. "

Sauce

    1 *15-oz can low-sodium or regular tomato sauce*

1 1/2 *Tbsp granulated sugar*

1 1/2 *Tbsp cider vinegar*

    1/2 *tsp minced garlic*

    1/2 *tsp dry mustard powder*

    1/4 *tsp dried thyme leaves*

    1/8 *tsp ground cloves*

    1/8 *tsp black pepper*

Chicken, vegetables, and buns

    3/4 *lb skinless, boneless chicken breast, cubed*

    1 *Tbsp olive oil*

    1 *Tbsp fat-free low-sodium or regular chicken broth*

    1 *large onion, chopped*

    1 *green bell pepper, seeded and chopped*

    4 *whole-wheat hamburger buns, toasted*

Prep Time: 20 minutes

Servings: 4

Serving Size: 1 cup, plus 1 (1 1/2 oz) hamburger bun

Exchanges
2 Starch
2 Vegetable
2 Very Lean Meat
1 Fat

Calories 335
   Calories from Fat 69
Total Fat . . . . .8 g
   Saturated Fat . . . . .1 g
Cholesterol . . . . .52 mg
Sodium . . . . .326 mg
Total Carbohydrate . . . .41 g
   Dietary Fiber . . . . .4 g
   Sugars . . . . .18 g
Protein . . . . .24 g

1 In a small non-reactive bowl, mix all the sauce ingredients together. Reserve.

2 In a large nonstick skillet, cook the chicken in the oil and broth, stirring frequently, until the chicken turns white.

3 Remove the chicken to a medium bowl. Add the onion and green pepper, and cook, stirring frequently, until onions are softened, about 6 or 7 minutes.

4 Return the chicken to the skillet. Add the sauce. Stir to mix well. Bring to a boil. Reduce the heat, cover, and cook 12 to 15 minutes or until chicken is cooked through. Serve open faced on toasted hamburger buns.

CHICKEN TORTILLA ROLL-UPS

For convenience, you can make these roll-ups several hours ahead of time, store them in the refrigerator, and heat them in the microwave or the oven just before serving.

1 cup frozen broccoli, corn, and red pepper medley

4 8-inch whole-wheat flour tortillas

1 cup nonfat refried beans

1/2 cup mild salsa

1/2 tsp chili powder

3 oz cooked chicken breast meat (3/4 cup diced)

1/2 cup shredded fat-free cheddar or Monterey Jack cheese

Fat-free sour cream for garnish (optional)

PREP TIME: 15 MINUTES

SERVINGS: 4

SERVING SIZE: 1 TORTILLA WITH FILLING

Exchanges
2 Starch
2 Vegetable
1 1/2 Lean Meat

Calories 280
   Calories from Fat 36
Total Fat . . . . .4 g
   Saturated Fat . . . . .0 g
Cholesterol . . . . .20 mg
Sodium . . . . .919 mg
Total Carbohydrate . . . .40 g
   Dietary Fiber . . . . .7 g
   Sugars . . . . .4 g
Protein . . . . .21 g

1 Cook the vegetables according to package directions. Drain in a colander, and set aside.

2 Meanwhile, for each roll-up, lay a tortilla on a plate or nonstick spray-coated baking sheet. With the back of a tablespoon, spread each tortilla with refried beans, dividing evenly, leaving a half-inch rim around the edge of the tortilla. In a small bowl, mix the salsa with chili powder. Spread the salsa mixture over beans, dividing evenly. Arrange meat in the center of the tortilla, dividing evenly. Top with vegetables, dividing evenly. Sprinkle with cheese, dividing evenly.

3 Fold in the right and left ends of each tortilla 1/2 inch to partially cover the interior mixture. Roll along the end closest to you until the mixture is completely covered, ending with rounded edge down.

4 To heat individually, put each tortilla on a plate, cover with wax paper, and microwave 2 minutes at high power. Or bake all 4 tortillas in a 350-degree oven for 15 minutes until the cheese is melted. Garnish with sour cream, if desired.

HOT SLICED SAUSAGE SANDWICHES WITH SWEET PEPPER AND ONION

The lower-fat turkey sausage works well in these hearty, very tasty sausage sandwiches. Since the filling is somewhat "saucy," you may want to serve the sandwiches on plates along with knives and forks. If possible, choose a brand of sausage with a maximum of 5 grams of fat for a 2-ounce serving portion.

1 14- to 16-oz package frozen sweet pepper and onion stir-fry or similar vegetable medley

1 Tbsp canola or olive oil

12 oz lower-fat smoked turkey sausage (such as kielbasa-flavored), cut diagonally into 1/4 inch–thick slices

1 8-oz package sliced, fresh mushrooms

2 cups bottled pasta sauce, preferably reduced sodium

1 tsp dried thyme leaves or oregano leaves (optional)

Pinch hot red pepper flakes (optional)

5 whole-wheat or multi-grain soft Kaiser or similar sandwich rolls

2 cups coarsely chopped romaine or escarole for garnish (optional)

PREP TIME: 15 MINUTES

SERVINGS: 5

SERVING SIZE: 1 CUP SANDWICH FILLING, PLUS 1 KAISER ROLL

Exchanges
3 1/2 Starch
2 Vegetable
1 High-Fat Meat
1 Fat

Calories 441
    Calories from Fat . . .117
Total Fat . . . . .13 g
    Saturated Fat . . . . .2 g
Cholesterol . . . . .24 mg
Sodium . . . . .933 mg
Total Carbohydrate . . . .63 g
    Dietary Fiber . . . . .7 g
    Sugars . . . . .21 g
Protein . . . . .18 g

1 Rinse the vegetables under hot water until thawed, then drain thoroughly. Pat dry with paper towels.

2 In a 12-inch, deep-sided nonstick skillet over high heat, combine the oil, vegetables, sausage slices, and mushrooms. Cook, stirring frequently, for 6 to 9 minutes, or until the excess liquid has evaporated from the pan and the sausage slices are beginning to brown.

3 Lower the heat to medium-high. Stir in the pasta sauce, thyme, and hot pepper flakes. Reduce the heat so the mixture simmers gently. Cook, stirring frequently, 6 to 8 minutes longer or until the sauce cooks down and has some body.

4 Spoon the filling into the roll bottoms, dividing it equally among them. Top the filling with the chopped romaine (if using). Add the roll tops. Serve immediately.

BEEFY PITA POCKETS

" Serve these hearty, hot sandwiches for lunch or dinner. "

FILLING

    3/4 *lb ground beef round*

    1 *cup chopped onion*

    1 *red bell pepper, seeded and diced*

    1 *7 3/4-oz can chickpeas, drained*

    1/2 *cup low-sodium or regular tomato sauce*

    1 *Tbsp apple cider vinegar*

    1 *Tbsp sugar*

    1 *tsp dried thyme leaves*

    1 *tsp dried marjoram leaves*

    1/4 *tsp ground cinnamon*

    Dash *ground cloves*

    3/4 *tsp salt, or to taste (optional)*

    1/4 *tsp black pepper*

BREAD

    4 *medium whole-wheat pita loaves, cut in half*

PREP TIME: 15 MINUTES

SERVINGS: 4

SERVING SIZE: 1 CUP FILLING, PLUS 1 6-INCH PITA LOAF

Exchanges
2 1/2 Starch
2 Lean Meat
2 Vegetable

Calories 345
  Calories from Fat 45
Total Fat . . . . .5 g
  Saturated Fat . . . . .1 g
Cholesterol . . . . .43 mg
Sodium . . . . .218 mg
Total Carbohydrate . . . .52 g
  Dietary Fiber . . . . .7 g
  Sugars . . . . .12 g
Protein . . . . .27 g

1 In a medium saucepan over medium heat, cook the beef, onion, and red pepper, stirring frequently, until the beef is browned and the onion is tender, about 5 or 6 minutes.

2 Add the chickpeas, tomato sauce, vinegar, sugar, thyme, marjoram, cinnamon, cloves, salt, if using, and black pepper. Bring to a simmer. Reduce the heat, and simmer uncovered 5 or 6 minutes until flavors are blended.

3 Gently spoon mixture into pita pockets, being careful not to overfill them.

GRILLED BEEF AND VEGETABLE SANDWICH

You'll love the flavor of these marinated flank steak sandwiches. Serve them open faced and eat with a knife and fork.

MARINADE AND MEAT

- 1/3 cup lemon juice
- 1/4 cup fat-free low-sodium or regular chicken broth
- 3 Tbsp canola or olive oil
- 1 Tbsp instant minced onions
- 2 tsp minced garlic
- 1 Tbsp salt-free Italian seasoning
- 1/4 tsp salt, or to taste (optional)
- 3/4 lb flank steak, trimmed of fat

VEGETABLES AND BREAD

- 3 Tbsp fat-free low-sodium or regular chicken broth
- 2 tsp canola oil or olive oil
- 2 medium bell peppers, preferably red or yellow and green, seeded and cut into 1/2-inch slices
- 1 medium onion, thinly sliced
- 1/2 tsp salt-free Italian seasoning
- 4 Italian plum tomatoes
- 1 loaf Italian bread

PREP TIME: 20 MINUTES

SERVINGS: 6

SERVING SIZE: 1
OPEN-FACED SANDWICH

Exchanges
2 1/2 Starch
1 Vegetable
2 Medium-Fat Meat

Calories 357
  Calories from Fat 81
Total Fat . . . . .9 g
  Saturated Fat . . . . .2 g
Cholesterol . . . . .24 mg
Sodium . . . . .496 mg
Total Carbohydrate . . . .45 g
  Dietary Fiber . . . . .4 g
  Sugars . . . . .5 g
Protein . . . . .24 g

1 In a small bowl, combine the lemon juice, broth, oil, onions, garlic, Italian seasoning, and salt, if desired. Stir to mix well. Lay the meat in a shallow glass baking dish. Add the marinade, and spoon some over the meat. Cover with plastic wrap, and refrigerate 8 hours or up to 24 hours, turning the meat once or twice and spooning marinade over it.

2 Adjust the rack 5 inches from the broiler. Preheat the broiler. Lift the meat out of the marinade with a large fork, and shake it lightly to remove excess marinade. Transfer the meat to a nonstick spray-coated broiler pan. Broil meat 5 inches from heat for 12 to 18 minutes, turning once, until desired degree of doneness is reached.

3 Meanwhile, in a nonstick skillet, combine the broth, oil, peppers, and onion. Sprinkle evenly with Italian seasoning. Cook over medium-high heat, stirring frequently, 7 to 9 minutes, until the onions and peppers are cooked. Stir in the tomatoes, and cook briefly (or leave tomatoes uncooked).

4 To serve, slice the meat on the diagonal and reserve. Cut the bread loaf in half crosswise and lengthwise to form 6 flat pieces. Lightly toast under the boiler. For each sandwich, lay a bread quarter on an individual plate. Divide the meat evenly among the bread halves. Top with the pepper, onion, and tomato mixture.

Smoked Salmon-Veggie Wraps

Fans of smoked salmon will love this interesting twist on the tortilla wrap sandwich. The salmon filling may be made well ahead, but the "sandwiches" need to be assembled shortly before serving time or they will become soggy. A food processor makes preparing the salmon filling a snap.

1 small celery stalk, very coarsely chopped

1 small carrot, very coarsely chopped

1/3 cup very coarsely chopped cauliflower florets

2 Tbsp coarsely chopped red or green bell pepper

3 Tbsp chopped green onions or fresh chives

2/3 cup fat-free cream cheese spread

3 oz smoked salmon, coarsely chopped

1 peeled medium cucumber, cut lengthwise into very thin slices

2 medium tomatoes, very thinly sliced

4 6-inch whole-wheat or regular flour tortillas

8 to 12 lettuce leaves

PREP TIME: 15 MINUTES

SERVINGS: 4

SERVING SIZE: 1 6-INCH TORTILLA WRAP SANDWICH

Exchanges
2 Starch
1 Vegetable
1 Medium-Fat Meat

Calories	241
Calories from Fat	45
Total Fat	5 g
Saturated Fat	0 g
Cholesterol	3 mg
Sodium	418 mg
Total Carbohydrate	33 g
Dietary Fiber	5 g
Sugars	6 g
Protein	16 g

1 In a food processor, combine the celery, carrot, cauliflower, bell pepper, and green onion (or chives). Process in on/off pulses until finely chopped. Sprinkle dollops of cream cheese and the salmon over the vegetables. Process in on/off pulses until the cream cheese is smoothly and evenly incorporated. The filling may be used immediately or refrigerated, airtight, for up to 48 hours.

2 Shortly before serving time, lay out the cucumber and tomato slices and lettuce leaves between paper towels; pat down the towels to remove excess moisture.

3 Dividing the filling equally (a generous 1/3 cup per wrap), spread it evenly over the surface of the tortillas, to within 1/2 inch of the edge. Lay the cucumber slices over the filling, patting them down. Arrange the tomato slices over the cucumber slices. Lay the lettuce leaves over the tomatoes, patching and tearing as necessary, to evenly cover the tortilla surface. Press down the leaves to compact the ingredients as much as possible.

4 Fold up one side of a tortilla about 3/4 inch to form a lip that holds in the filling. Then, working from the perpendicular sides, fold over the tortilla to enclose the filling. Repeat with remaining tortillas.

5 Serve immediately or refrigerate 5 or 10 minutes to allow flavors to blend; for best texture do not store longer.

TUNA MELT SANDWICHES

This updated version of a sandwich classic has zippy flavor, appealing color, and a crispy-soft texture. It's great for a hurry-up meal.

2 6-oz cans water-packed solid white albacore tuna, well rinsed and drained

1 1/4 cups finely chopped celery

2 Tbsp finely chopped dill pickles or dill pickle relish

1/4 cup reduced-fat mayonnaise

2 Tbsp chopped fresh chives or finely chopped green onion

2 tsp Dijon or Dijon-style mustard

2 tsp apple cider vinegar or red wine vinegar

1/8 tsp black pepper (optional)

5 large slices crusty 100 percent multi-grained bread or whole-wheat bread

2/3 cup (about 2 1/2 oz) shredded or grated fat-free cheddar cheese

PREP TIME: 15 MINUTES

SERVINGS: 5

SERVING SIZE: 1 OPEN-FACE SANDWICH

Exchanges
1 Starch
3 Very Lean Meat
1 Fat

Calories 211
  Calories from Fat 63
Total Fat . . . . .7 g
  Saturated Fat . . . . .1 g
Cholesterol . . . . .35 mg
Sodium . . . . .617 mg
Total Carbohydrate . . . .13 g
  Dietary Fiber . . . . .3 g
  Sugars . . . . .3 g
Protein . . . . .24 g

1 Preheat the broiler to 500 degrees.

2 Combine the tuna, celery, pickle, mayonnaise, chives, mustard, vinegar, and pepper (if using) in a large bowl; stir well.

3 Spread the tuna mixture on the bread, dividing it equally among the slices. Lay the slices on a foil-lined broiler pan, slightly apart. Sprinkle cheese over each sandwich.

4 Broil about 4 inches from the broiler until the cheese melts and browns and the bread is crusty, 2 to 3 minutes.

VEGETARIAN PITA POCKETS

"Since we have vegetarian friends and family members, we're always on the lookout for dishes we can serve them, such as this pita pocket variation."

FILLING

1 cup chopped onion

1 cup coarsely chopped cauliflower florets

1/2 large sweet red pepper, seeded and chopped

2 Tbsp olive oil

1 8-oz can chickpeas, drained

1/4 cup dark raisins

1/2 cup reduced-sodium or regular tomato sauce

1 Tbsp apple cider vinegar

1 tsp dried thyme leaves

1/2 tsp ground cumin

3/4 tsp salt, or to taste (optional)

1/4 tsp black pepper

BREAD

2 medium whole-wheat pita loaves, cut in half

PREP TIME: 15 MINUTES

SERVINGS: 4

SERVING SIZE:
1/2 GENEROUS CUP FILLING, PLUS
1/2 6-INCH PITA LOAF

Exchanges
1 1/2 Starch
1/2 Fruit
2 Vegetable
1 1/2 Fat

Calories 251
   Calories from Fat 72
Total Fat . . . . .8 g
   Saturated Fat . . . . .1 g
Cholesterol . . . . .0 mg
Sodium . . . . .141 mg
Total Carbohydrate . . . .41 g
   Dietary Fiber . . . . .6 g
   Sugars . . . . .14 g
Protein . . . . .8 g

1 In a medium saucepan over medium heat, cook onion, cauliflower, and red pepper in olive oil, stirring frequently, until onion is tender, about 5 or 6 minutes.

2 Add chickpeas, raisins, tomato sauce, vinegar, thyme, cumin, salt, if desired, and black pepper. Bring to a simmer. Reduce heat to medium low, and simmer uncovered 5 or 6 minutes until flavors are blended.

3 Gently spoon mixture into pita pockets, being careful not to overfill them.

VEGETARIAN TORTILLA ROLL-UPS

You can make these roll-ups several hours ahead of time, store them in the refrigerator, and heat them up in the microwave or the oven just before serving.

1 1/2 cups frozen broccoli, corn, and
   red pepper

4 8-inch whole-wheat flour tortillas

1 cup fat-free refried beans

1/2 cup mild salsa

1 cup diced fresh tomatoes,
   drained in a sieve

1/2 tsp chili powder

1/2 tsp ground cumin

1 cup shredded fat-free cheddar cheese

Reduced-fat sour cream for
garnish (optional)

PREP TIME: 15 MINUTES

SERVINGS: 4

SERVING SIZE: 1 TORTILLA
   WITH FILLING

Exchanges
3 1/2 Starch
1 Vegetable
1 Lean Meat

Calories 271
   Calories from Fat 27
Total Fat . . . . .3 g
   Saturated Fat . . . . .0 g
Cholesterol . . . . .5 mg
Sodium . . . . .887 mg
Total Carbohydrate . . . .42 g
   Dietary Fiber . . . . .8 g
   Sugars . . . . .5 g
Protein . . . . .19 g

1 Cook the vegetables according to package directions without added fat or salt. Drain in a colander, and set aside.

2 Meanwhile, for each roll-up, lay a tortilla on a flat surface. With the back of a tablespoon, spread each tortilla with refried beans, dividing evenly, leaving a half-inch rim around the edge of the tortilla.

3 In a small bowl, mix the salsa and tomatoes with chili powder and cumin. Spread the salsa mixture over the beans, dividing evenly. Arrange the vegetables in center of the tortilla, dividing evenly. Sprinkle with cheese, dividing evenly.

4 Fold in the right and left ends of the tortilla just enough to cover the edges of the interior mixture. Roll along the end closest to you until the mixture is completely covered, ending with rounded edge down.

5 To heat individually, place each tortilla on a plate, cover with wax paper, and microwave 2 minutes at high power. Or bake all 4 tortillas on a nonstick spray-coated baking sheet in a 350-degree oven for 15 minutes until the cheese is melted. Garnish with sour cream, if desired.

QUICK HUMMUS-VEGGIE WRAPS

Hummus is a very flavorful and zesty Mediterranean spread featuring ground chickpeas, garlic, and olive and sesame oils. If you usually make your own hummus it will work fine in this recipe, but we find commercial hummus a convenient (and quite tasty) time-saver and call for it here. We prefer the "traditional-flavor" hummus over the more exotically seasoned versions, and we also look for brands that contain only olive oil and tahini (sesame oil). These easy hummus-veggie wraps are a great substitute for the usual sandwich—they can be made ahead and pack well—and will please vegetarians and non-vegetarians alike.

2/3 cup (a 5 to 6-oz container) hummus

2 10-inch flour tortillas

1 small celery stalk, finely chopped

1 small carrot, finely grated or chopped

2 or 3 green onions, including tender tops, chopped (optional)

1 medium tomato, very thinly sliced

4 or 5 medium iceberg or other sturdy lettuce leaves

PREP TIME: 10 MINUTES

SERVINGS: 4

SERVING SIZE: 1/2 OF A
10-INCH TORTILLA WRAP

Exchanges
2 Starch
1 Vegetable
1 Fat

Calories 207
　Calories from Fat 56
Total Fat . . . . .6 g
　Saturated Fat . . . . .1 g
Cholesterol . . . . .0 mg
Sodium . . . . .287 mg
Total Carbohydrate . . . .33 g
　Dietary Fiber . . . . .5 g
　Sugars . . . . .5 g
Protein . . . . .6 g

1 Spread a scant 1/3 cup hummus evenly over the surface of each tortilla, to within 1/4 inch of the edge. Sprinkle half the celery, carrots, and green onion (if desired) over each tortilla.

2 Blot the tomato slices and lettuce leaves dry on paper towels. Arrange the tomato slices over the tortillas so the surface is covered to within 1/4 inch of the edges. Lay the lettuce leaves over the tomatoes, patching and tearing as necessary, to cover the tortilla surface to within 1/4 inch of the edges. Press down the leaves to compact the vegetables as much as possible.

3 Working from one side, tightly roll up one tortilla to enclose the filling. Repeat with remaining tortilla. If not serving the wraps right away, roll up each one tightly in wax paper; twist the ends to keep the paper from unrolling. Then refrigerate for up to 36 hours.

4 At serving time, unwrap the tortillas (if wrapped). On a slight diagonal with a large sharp knife, cut each tortilla in half crosswise to form two wrap sandwiches.

BLACK-BEAN FAJITA WRAPS

These wraps make a great hurry-up lunch or supper. The wraps can also be made well ahead for a meal with absolutely no waiting at all.

    1 14- to 15-oz can black beans,
      rinsed and drained

    1/3 cup mild to hot thick-and-
        chunky salsa or picante sauce

    2 or 3 green onions, including tender
           tops, chopped

    2 10-inch flour tortillas

    1/2 cup grated or shredded reduced-fat
        cheddar or Monterey Jack cheese

    1/3 cup coarsely chopped cilantro leaves

    1 large tomato, very thinly sliced

    4 or 5 medium iceberg lettuce leaves or other
           sturdy lettuce leaves

PREP TIME: 15 MINUTES

SERVINGS: 4

SERVING SIZE: 1/2 OF A
    10-INCH TORTILLA WRAP

Exchanges
2 1/2 Starch
1 Vegetable
1 Fat

Calories 269
    Calories from Fat 56
Total Fat . . . . .6 g
    Saturated Fat . . . . .2 g
Cholesterol . . . . .10 mg
Sodium . . . . .443 mg
Total Carbohydrate . . . .41 g
    Dietary Fiber . . . . . . .9 g
    Sugars . . . . .5 g
Protein . . . . .14 g

1 In a medium, non-reactive bowl, combine the beans, salsa, and green onions, mixing with a fork. Mash enough beans to yield a paste or spread-like consistency.

2 Spread half the bean mixture over the surface of each tortilla, to within 1/4 inch of the edge. Sprinkle half the cheese and cilantro over each tortilla.

3 Blot the tomato slices and lettuce leaves dry on paper towels. Arrange the tomato slices over the tortillas so the surface is covered to within 1/4 inch of the edges. Lay the lettuce leaves over the tomatoes, patching and tearing as necessary, to cover the tortilla surface to within 1/4 inch of the edges.

4 Working from one side, neatly roll up one tortilla to enclose the filling. Repeat with remaining tortilla. If not serving the wraps immediately, roll up each one in wax paper; twist the ends to keep the paper from unrolling. Then refrigerate for up to 8 hours.

5 At serving time unwrap the tortillas (if wrapped). Using a sharp knife, on a slight diagonal cut each tortilla in half crosswise to form two wrap sandwiches.

PORTOBELLO MUSHROOM SANDWICHES

Portobellos taste surprisingly meaty when marinated, broiled, and tucked in sandwiches. For best flavor use a good, hearty bread such as a coarse-textured, mixed-grain loaf or a crusty, wheat sourdough.

2 1/2 Tbsp olive oil, plus
    1/2 Tbsp for brushing
    mushroom cap tops

1 1/2 Tbsp fresh lemon juice

1 tsp balsamic vinegar

3/4 tsp dried thyme leaves

1/8 to 1/4 tsp black pepper

Scant 1/2 tsp salt

3 large portobello mushrooms
    (about 5 oz each, untrimmed), stems
    removed

8 slices crusty mixed-grain or sourdough
    bread

4 slices fat-free mozzarella or provolone
    cheese

1 large tomato, thinly sliced

1 7-oz jar roasted red sweet peppers, very
    well drained and cut into pieces, if
    necessary

1 cup alfalfa sprouts

Thinly sliced red onion rings for garnish
(optional)

PREP TIME: 20 MINUTES

SERVINGS: 4

SERVING SIZE: 1 SANDWICH

Exchanges
2 Starch
1 Vegetable
2 Medium-Fat Meat

Calories 328
    Calories from Fat . . .108
Total Fat . . . . .12 g
    Saturated Fat . . . . . . .2 g
Cholesterol . . . . .5 mg
Sodium . . . . .617 mg
Total Carbohydrate . . . .36 g
    Dietary Fiber . . . . . . .9 g
    Sugars . . . . .10 g
Protein . . . . .19 g

Handy Tip

If desired, you can marinate, broil, and slice the mushrooms ahead, then simply re-warm them when ready to put together the sandwiches.

1 For the marinade: in a small non-reactive bowl, stir together the 2 1/2 table-spoons oil, lemon juice, balsamic vinegar, thyme, pepper, and salt until well blended. Rub the smooth sides (tops) of the mushroom caps lightly with a little more olive oil. Place the mushroom caps smooth-side down (gills up) in a non-reactive dish large enough to hold them. Drizzle the marinade into the mushroom caps, dividing it equally among them. Let them stand and marinate, uncovered, at least 10 minutes and up to 30 minutes.

2 Adjust the oven rack to about 4 inches from the broiler element. Set the broiler to the highest setting and preheat for about 5 minutes. Arrange the mushroom caps, gill side up, on a broiler pan or on a heavy-duty rimmed baking sheet.

3 Broil the mushrooms about 6 to 8 minutes, or until tender through when tested in the thickest part with a fork. Working on a cutting board, slice the caps on the bias into 1/4-inch thick slices.

4 Lay the slices of bread on the broiler pan used for the mushrooms. Divide the mushroom slices among the bread slices, then top each with a slice of mozzarella or provolone, on each of the 4 slices of bread. Turn off the broiler. Return the broiler pan to the broiler just until the cheese partially melts, about 30 seconds. Immediately remove from the broiler.

5 Cover the cheese on each sandwich with tomato slices, roasted pepper, alfalfa sprouts, red onion rings (if using), and a second slice of bread, patting down slightly. Cut the sandwiches in half using a large sharp knife. Serve immediately.

Sloppy Joes

Here's a spiced-up version of an old favorite.

> 3/4 lb extra-lean ground beef
> 1 medium onion, chopped
> 1/2 large green bell pepper, seeded and chopped
> 1 medium celery rib, sliced
> 1 15-oz can low-sodium or regular tomato sauce
> 2 Tbsp cider vinegar
> 2 Tbsp Splenda
> 1 tsp dried thyme leaves
> 1 large bay leaf
> 1/4 tsp ground cinnamon
> 1/8 tsp ground cloves
> 1/4 tsp salt (optional)
> Dash black pepper
> 4 whole-wheat or regular hamburger buns, toasted

1 In a Dutch oven or similar large, heavy pot, combine the ground beef, onion, green pepper, and celery. Cook over medium heat, stirring frequently, until the beef is browned.

2 Add the tomato sauce, vinegar, Splenda, thyme, bay leaf, cinnamon, cloves, salt, if desired, and pepper. Bring to a boil. Reduce heat, cover, and simmer 15 to 20 minutes until flavors are well blended. Remove bay leaf. Serve open faced over toasted hamburger buns.

Prep Time: 12 minutes

Servings: 4

Serving Size: 1 cup meat mixture, plus 1 hamburger bun

Exchanges
2 Starch
1 Vegetable
2 Lean Meat

Calories 286
    Calories from Fat 54
Total Fat . . . . .6 g
    Saturated Fat . . . . .2 g
Cholesterol . . . . .45 mg
Sodium . . . . .281 mg
Total Carbohydrate . . . .36 g
    Dietary Fiber . . . . .6 g
    Sugars . . . . .6 g
Protein . . . . .22 g

ALPHABETICAL LIST OF RECIPES

Subject Index

Beef

Other Titles Available from the American Diabetes Association

The Complete Quick & Hearty Diabetic Cookbook, 2nd Edition

by American Diabetes Association

Enjoy all of the home style meals you love brought back in healthy and tasty versions! Completely updated to feature the latest ADA nutrition recommendations, these recipes are better than ever. Make this classic an addition to your cooking library.
Order no. 4624-02; Price: $15.95

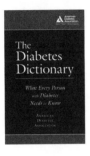

The Diabetes Dictionary

by American Diabetes Association

To stay healthy, you need to understand the constantly growing vocabulary of diabetes research and treatment. This gives you the straightforward definitions of diabetes terms and concepts you need. With more than 500 entries, this affordable, pocket-size book is an indispensable resource for every person with diabetes.
Order no. 5020-01; Price $5.95

Diabetes Fit Food

by Ellen Haas

Put tasteless, boring recipes in the past with this new cookbook from healthy-eating expert Ellen Haas. She has compiled amazing, healthy recipes from some of America's best celebrity chefs, including Todd English, Alice Waters, and others. Finally, you can make sensible, healthy eating taste like it comes from a five-star restaurant.
Order no. 4661-01; Price $16.95

American Diabetes Association Complete Guide to Diabetes, 4th Edition

by American Diabetes Association

Have all the information on diabetes that you need close at hand. The world's largest collection of diabetes self-care tips, techniques, and tricks for solving diabetes-related problems is back in its fourth edition, and it's bigger and better than ever before.
Order no. 4809-04; Price $29.95

To order these and other great American Diabetes Association titles, call 1-800-232-6733 or visit *http://store.diabetes.org*. American Diabetes Association titles are also available in bookstores nationwide.

About the American Diabetes Association

The American Diabetes Association is the nation's leading voluntary health organization supporting diabetes research, information, and advocacy. Its mission is to prevent and cure diabetes and to improve the lives of all people affected by diabetes. The American Diabetes Association is the leading publisher of comprehensive diabetes information. Its huge library of practical and authoritative books for people with diabetes covers every aspect of self-care—cooking and nutrition, fitness, weight control, medications, complications, emotional issues, and general self-care.

To join the American Diabetes Association: Call 1-800-806-7801 or log on to www.diabetes.org/membership

For more information about diabetes or ADA programs and services: Call 1-800-342-2383. E-mail: AskADA@diabetes.org or log on to www.diabetes.org

To locate an ADA/NCQA Recognized Provider of quality diabetes care in your area: www.ncqa.org/dprp

To find an ADA Recognized Education Program in your area: Call 1-800-342-2383. www.diabetes.org/for-health-professionals-and-scientists/recognition/edrecognition.jsp

To join the fight to increase funding for diabetes research, end discrimination, and improve insurance coverage: Call 1-800-342-2383. www.diabetes.org/advocacy-and-legalresources/advocacy.jsp

To find out how you can get involved with the programs in your community: Call 1-800-342-2383. See below for program Web addresses.

- American Diabetes Month: educational activities aimed at those diagnosed with diabetes—month of November. www.diabetes.org/communityprograms-and-localevents/americandiabetesmonth.jsp
- American Diabetes Alert: annual public awareness campaign to find the undiagnosed—held the fourth Tuesday in March. www.diabetes.org/communityprograms-and-localevents/americandiabetesalert.jsp
- American Diabetes Association Latino Initiative: diabetes awareness program targeted to the Latino community. www.diabetes.org/communityprograms-and-localevents/latinos.jsp
- African American Program: diabetes awareness program targeted to the African American community. www.diabetes.org/communityprograms-and-localevents/africanamericans.jsp
- Awakening the Spirit: Pathways to Diabetes Prevention & Control: diabetes awareness program targeted to the Native American community. www.diabetes.org/communityprograms-and-localevents/nativeamericans.jsp

To find out about an important research project regarding type 2 diabetes: www.diabetes.org/diabetes-research/research-home.jsp

To obtain information on making a planned gift or charitable bequest: Call 1-888-700-7029. www.wpg.cc/stl/CDA/homepage/1,1006,509,00.html

To make a donation or memorial contribution: Call 1-800-342-2383. www.diabetes.org/support-the-cause/make-a-donation.jsp